ADVANCE PRAISE FOR *TIP OF THE SPEAR*

"*Tip of the Spear* is not another SEAL autobiography. Author Rodney Magallan provides an accessible life philosophy illustrated by his impressive experiences working toward and operating at the tip of the spear. Reading *Tip of the Spear* is like having a deep conversation over a whiskey with a close friend who will give it to you straight and not accept any excuses. For civilians like myself who have always been in awe of individuals like Rodney, *Tip of the Spear* offers a straightforward, no-nonsense philosophy that allows anyone to access greatness wherever they are within their careers, companies, and relationships. This book is for any person who ever believed they are capable of more."

—**Evan Prive-Shereck**,
President/Co-Founder of L.A.G. Tactical Inc.

"Let me start by saying that I am not the type of person who would pick up a book like this from the shelf—which is *precisely* why I find Rodney Magallan to be so brilliant. This isn't another 'cool tactical guy' book made for other folks who have served our country. No, Rodney takes the lessons he learned out in the field and shares them for the average reader to digest and grow from, all while enveloping said lessons with the wildest stories you've ever read. Half the time I was reading this, I couldn't believe that this was somebody's real life, let alone the true experiences of someone who seems so incredibly pleasant and giving. Rodney clearly has a mission to educate a new generation of people—a generation more isolated via technology than ever—sharing hard lessons from the field that will fundamentally change how you think about life and yourself. It is a deeply empowering read. If you're looking for something to get you inspired again, this is the book for you. I mean it. Thank me later."

—**Sheila Houlahan,**
Actress, Award-Winning Producer

"Having fortunately served with Rodney, I personally know his actions have directly saved many lives and missions. Anyone who knows him knows he walks the walk and talks the talk, and they will follow him anywhere because he's been there, done that. Clique aside, we would follow Rodney anywhere. We have a saying in the Teams: 'Learn from others' mistakes—you might not survive your own.' Rodney's advice comes from hard-earned experience at the tip of the spear. TAKE IT!"

—**Wook,**
Navy SEAL Captain (Retired)

"In a world brimming with leadership advice and theories, it's truly rare to find a book that combines wisdom, authenticity, and insights in such a profound way. Rodney weaves his fantastic life story and military history into an insightful book on leadership. What distinguishes this book is its emphasis on real-world experience gained over the years in numerous high-risk professions. Some of you may have never heard of Rodney; he takes perverse pride in that fact. Rodney's book is not about showcasing his achievements but empowering others and sharing his knowledge. His genuine passion for this mission is evident, and I can personally attest to the value of his teachings. From time in a team room, downrange, or completing a complex task, Rodney was always the first to volunteer or give sage advice. Rodney is the steel that sharpens other steel. The reader of this book is presented with a rare opportunity to learn from a truly silent professional."

—**James Rusk,**
Director of Risk Management, Gates Family Office

"*Tip of the Spear* takes an often overused analogy and applies it in a way that is unique, refreshing, and a bit surprising. Dropping the political affectations and niceties that muddle the message in so many books of this generation, Rodney offers a blunt reality check to help people find their proper place in any organization beyond the specific titles and apparent prestige. He clearly demonstrates how that place will, and should, change as priorities and life demands evolve—and how that is okay. He shows that every position is vital, so the key is to make sure your job matches your goals and be the best at it—unapologetically and with no excuses. This is a must-read for anyone at a major decision point in their life or who is preparing for one."

—**David Shavell**,
Senior Intelligence Officer

"As a former SEAL officer turned family man and business owner, I've read countless books on leadership and self-improvement, but none have resonated with me like this one. Rodney's masterful storytelling and profound insights have elevated the way I understand the intricate dance of teamwork and leadership. His words cut through the noise, bringing simplicity and clarity to the most challenging concepts.

Rodney's ability to distill complex ideas into engaging and memorable stories is nothing short of genius. From the first page, you're drawn into a narrative that not only captivates the mind but also speaks to the heart. He brilliantly unpacks the essential truth that understanding oneself is the cornerstone of effective leadership.

This book is a treasure trove for anyone striving to unlock their potential and lead with confidence. Whether you're looking to deepen your self-awareness or enhance your leadership skills, Rodney provides the roadmap with wisdom, humor, and authenticity. This isn't just a book you read; it's a journey you embark on. Missing out on this would be a disservice to your personal and professional growth."

—**Jared Ogden**,
Former Navy SEAL and CEO of Triumph Systems

TIP OF THE SPEAR

IT'S NOT WHAT YOU THINK

RODNEY MAGALLAN

Ballast Books, LLC
www.ballastbooks.com

Copyright © 2024 by Rodney Magallan

The views expressed in this publication are those of the author and do not necessarily reflect the official policy or position of the Department of Defense or the US government. The public release clearance of this publication by the Department of Defense does not imply Department of Defense endorsement or factual accuracy of the material.

ISBN: 978-1-964934-19-8 (Paperback)
ISBN: 978-1-964934-20-4 (Hardcover)
ISBN: 978-1-964934-21-1 (Ebook)

Printed in the United States of America

Published by Ballast Books
www.ballastbooks.com

For more information, bulk orders, appearances, or speaking requests, please email: info@ballastbooks.com

This book is dedicated to all those who make it their life's work to serve others as well as my friends, my family, and the teachers who believed I had it in me to write my own future. Last but certainly not least, I dedicate this book to my loving wife, daughter, and son. No words can describe the gratitude, pride, and love I have for them. They make me want to be a better version of myself every day. Thank you.

TABLE OF CONTENTS

FOREWORD

I have known Rodney Magallan, the author of the *Tip of the Spear*, since 1989. At the time, I was a junior officer on my second deployment. We were assigned to SEAL Team 4 Golf Platoon under Lt. Tom Casey, a legend inside the Teams who won the Navy Cross at Paitilla Airfield. Golf Platoon, which had two squads of eight men each, did a pre-deployment train-up and then headed to Panama for six months. Incidentally, we had a lot of "twos" back then: two officers, two non-commissioned leaders, two radiomen, two point men, two snipers, two jumpmasters, and two corpsmen, ad nauseam. Rodney was First Squad's sniper and corpsman. We spent a lot of time together traveling through Central and South America. It was a great time to be in the military!

Now, when I reflect back, I remember that we had great Navy SEALs, average Navy SEALs, and horrible Navy SEALs. I can recall the same about the platoons inside each SEAL Team; some were awesome, some were average, and many sucked. (Those generally comprised a bunch of clowns who told everyone in any bar they were Navy SEALs and who only cared about chasing women and partying on the government's dime; they couldn't fight their way out of a birthday party for kindergartners.) By my estimate, Golf Platoon was a great one with nine of its members selected for SEAL Team 6 and five of those going further to work with the CIA. Golf Platoon, simply put, always had character. The platoon had wit, humor, experience, eagerness to learn, strength, and competence—which mattered. I couldn't wait to head to work each morning.

When I dwell on my memories of that time over thirty years ago, I can't help but think about how much I miss the great Navy SEALs, the ones who mattered—the good ones. Those who were professional and serious, who tried to be the best versions of themselves as American fighters, frogmen, and operators. They didn't need to brag because they were driven by something more powerful, something that truly made a difference.

Of course, every shitty SEAL tells people they are awesome and incredible, even though they aren't. In fact, the crap frogmen brought everyone down all the time, especially on temporary duty trips and deployments. I know this from experience, as Golf Platoon had two misfits who drove us crazy with their continuous bullshit. This is the real stuff one never reads about in Navy SEAL books. To this day, I still regret having to deal with all the shit SEALs, the bull-shitters, the self-centered egotists and entitled elites.

But when Rodney asked me to review his book, which aims to tell the same thing I just went over but in a positive, not-in-your-face way . . . I wanted to help. I admired Rodney Magallan even as an E-5 back in 1990. He was awesome to work with. If I had to take my sixty-year-old body back to war, I would pick Rodney to go with me. The guy is funny and kind. He chased excellence in everything he did inside the Teams. Everyone who knew him and operated with him admired him and wanted him alongside if danger was coming. His experiences and history in the navy, in the CIA, and with the US Marshals should show for something. I read his book and enjoyed the "reflections" from Rodney.

I can still remember way back to 1990 in Central America when we were on a training event in the jungle. At the time, the Second Squad of Golf Platoon was lying in ambush along a jungle trail with blanks in our guns. The objective of the day was to run counter-ambush drills focusing on the point man, who always moved slowly to try to spot any hidden opponents. That jungle was so thick and dense, no point man ever spotted the other squads' ambush. Well, Rodney challenged the ambushing squad, saying he could get them to reveal themselves.

From my perfect locale along a jungle trail with my squad in an L-shaped ambush, we waited for our brothers in First Squad to patrol to us 'cause we knew their route in advance. Rodney was on point, moving slowly into my squad's kill zone, but it all went to hell in moments. Before I knew it, Second Squad blew it in the weirdest way. Vietnam taught the SEAL Teams jungle combat. We were all trained by Vietnam veterans and worked in the jungle for most of my time with SEAL Team 4. We all knew that any noise could give one away in the jungle and that silence was an operational imperative for survival.

So, back to the mock ambush and Golf Platoon's two squads going head to head. As I said, Second Squad blew it. We gave away our position too early, before the other squad had entered our fields of fire, before they were supposed to be under our collective eight gun sights. Luckily, we all messed up, meaning the eight-man squad all failed together at the exact same point. We did this by laughing our asses off.

As First Squad came down the trail with Rodney on point, it was his uniform that got our attention. He had his CAR-15 with M203 grenade launcher (back then, we used the Colt Model 727 rifle), boonie hat, web gear, and boots—with no clothes on at all. Just naked. I never even thought about something like that, yet he managed to pull it off so routinely.

Rodney wanted to win—that was all. He was not gonna be a closet nudist AND a conventional stay-inside-the-box thinker. So, he stripped off his uniform and then patrolled nude with complete dedication while methodically scanning the jungle in hopes of spotting Second Squad. I would have to confer with seven other dudes before speaking for the group, but I still believe that what got me to crack up was Rodney's face—his serious look while staring into the foliage. What a freaking knucklehead!

So, thirty-four years after that jungle laugh, I can tell you for a fact that Rodney can operate and that I miss those laughs and great times!

—Anonymous Navy SEAL officer who retired in 2010 after twenty-three years of service and seven operational deployments

INTRODUCTION

I am a man of many experiences and jobs. A lot of what I know and can do is directly attributed to my time working with the US government. Throughout my four decades of work experience—from migrant worker on public assistance as a teenager to Navy SEAL by age nineteen and then federal agent back to active naval service as a SEAL officer—I started to notice trends in how people think, especially in how people view their work or the position they hold. *Am I good enough? Do I have what it takes? I'm surprised I made it this far.*

I saw self-doubt prevent so many talented people from doing greater things. I also started to see confident, accomplished individuals in the workplace complain the most. Similar to those who doubted themselves, this mentality would hold them back from achieving their greatest potential because they somehow thought things were being done poorly or flat-out wrong.

Maybe it has always been this way and my eyes only began opening to this dynamic as I became responsible for more and more people. Or perhaps it is something cultural that created so much self-doubt and entitlement in our workforce today. Either way, as I enter a new chapter of life, I have this burning desire to share my personal journey from migrant worker to retired Navy SEAL commander and everything in between. I hope what I have to say helps anyone who is struggling in the workplace find answers to why things are as they are.

When it comes down to it, living the life of the elite is not what people think. It's hard work and sacrifice, and it doesn't stop. There's never a break until you're ready to remove yourself from that position. That being said, it's something anyone can do—if they're willing to live that kind of life and put that work and sacrifice in. The elite aren't "different." If you have the work ethic, you can do the same great things. If you think that you can't or that you have a different mentality, you hold yourself back.

Of course, not everyone can be at the tip of the spear. Being the best of the best isn't just a position—it's an attitude. A mindset. If you put the same tenacity into whatever it is you're doing, wherever you land in the pecking order, you can be just as successful.

The bottom line is that you should stop looking at these doctors, lawyers, CEOs, Navy SEALs, etc., as the only markers of success. We define our own success. You can still be elite at what your definition of success is.

As you read this book, it may be tempting to label me according to my job: "military hero" or "CIA operative" or "migrant worker." If a label must be placed on me, however, let it be "father," "husband," "brother," or "friend." Every job I've held was a means to an end. Whether it was to provide for my family or to find a way back to serve during a time of war, I did what I did with others in mind. I thank them for their silent motivation that kept me going.

Let's get after it.

Navy SEAL: *tape or wire placed on a container or space to restrict access.*

Just kidding! SEAL stands for sea, air, and land. We are the US Navy's commandos—sailors who conduct special operations for our country.

In the late 1980s, I was a young frogman, aka SEAL, on the East Coast. Occasionally, we were required to wear our dress uniforms, which included our navy warfare specialty pins. Other sailors on base outside of our community would constantly come up to us and ask, "What is that pin on your uniform?" I usually responded with, "I am a Navy SEAL," which generally garnered a blank stare in return. (Back then, few had heard of the SEALs, even within the military and especially in the civilian world.) Seeing the disconnect, I would explain that I was in the navy band and played the clarinet. This response was readily understandable because the band was stationed on the same base as the SEAL Team I was attached to. The response to that? "Oh!" And they would walk away.

"Navy band" was my answer for the Trident I wore on my uniform until I heard my buddy's brilliant response: "I'm a space shuttle M60 gunner." Just imagine the shuttle up in space. A guy in a space suit hanging out of a side door. Automatic belt-fed machine gun in tow. Looking for any and all space threats to the shuttle. It was clear to us we were being facetious, but people thought our silly response to their question was an actual job in the navy, which amused us greatly.

That, then, became my new go-to whenever I was asked what the Trident stood for.

Fast-forward to today and pretty much everyone in the US is now familiar with SEALs. Some even consider themselves experts on the subject (thanks, Hollywood). In fact, I honestly think that, overall, people in the United States know way more than they probably *should* about special operations and what all that can entail. Or they believe that they know a great deal about the how and why we do what we do without fully comprehending the extreme sacrifice required to operate at that level.

Movies and television often romanticize the idea of being a SEAL because the story needs to end in roughly 120 minutes. It's easy to respect the motive and drive people have to fight for something bigger than them. To live that kind of life, however, means you adopt and adhere to the core values of the elite. You give up a lot, and you have to count the cost daily. A common tagline we would use in the teams is, "The only easy day was yesterday."

Many like the idea of being at what most would consider the top of military engagement, but few are truly willing to lay it all down and give everything to get there.

There is a reason we—the special operation forces of the US military—are called the *tip of the spear.*

To start, I should tell you where my idea for this book first came from. When I made the decision to return to active duty, I knew that I was going to have to deploy as an officer in charge (OIC) in order to be competitive for promotion. An OIC is responsible for all the members of a platoon. This includes training of expected capabilities to be used during deployment, administrative issues of the platoon (including promotion exams, general military training, wills, pay issues, travel arrangements, power of attorney, etc.), good order and discipline of the platoon, general health of the platoon, equipment for the platoon, mission of the platoon when deployed, and so forth. And all this while maintaining your individual skills as a SEAL operator.

"So what?" say you?

Well, this would be my sixth deployment with the navy. I had three deployments with SEAL Team 4, four years with SEAL Team 6, three years at Special Boat Unit 20 helping stand up the maritime craft aerial delivery system (MCADS) program while going to night school and running a medical department under my belt. And not only that—I had served as a civilian as well, becoming a deputy US marshal for the Southern District of Texas, being recruited by the CIA Global Response Staff (GRS) after 9/11, providing protection in high-threat areas, and staying on in Naval Special Warfare reserves as an officer. When I was mobilized as a task unit commander in the Horn of Africa, I had been given twenty-nine days to report in. And when I came home from deployment, I returned to my wife and children and a civilian job.

Up to that point, I had been running *hard* for twenty-three years—fifty countries, many deployments, and multiple trips overseas for my civilian jobs. Subsequently, when I began to encounter young SEALs who were complaining about their second or third deployment as I prepared for my umpteenth, it honestly pissed me off a bit. Now don't get me wrong; sailors bitch (it's when they stop that you need to worry because now they are plotting), but these youngsters were lacking the vision of the bigger picture—giving it ALL to stay at the top.

When I joined the US Navy in 1985, I hadn't planned on becoming a SEAL. No one, including myself, even really knew what SEALs were at that time. Once I joined their ranks, however, this ideology of giving it all was a very common attitude among us. No one had to remind or motivate us to give 100 percent day in and day out. Quite frankly, most of us barely spoke about it—we just laid it all down at all times, pushing ourselves and each other to the limit, and staying laser focused on the mission in front of us. No discussion, no question. It just was.

If you are going to say you're the best, then you'd better be the best.

As I was getting ready for my sixth deployment for the navy as a forty-something-year-old man, I was taken aback by the twenty-year-olds complaining about having to do a workup. (A workup is usually six to eighteen months of training in preparation for the deployment.) I began to see this attitude more and more as I came back from that deployment and took the operations officer's position, which meant I wasn't just the head of operations for a single platoon but was in charge of operations for a whole team of platoons.

One day, I finally got fed up and told some young SEALs, "Y'all want to tell people you're the tip of the spear, but you don't want to do what it takes to BE the tip of the spear!"

Why that phrase? All of the US Military Special Operations Forces (SOF) are directed by Special Operations Command (SOCOM), and every month, SOCOM sends out a magazine titled *Tip of the Spear*, which highlights the accomplishments of each service's special operations around the globe. Our office spaces always had many issues of this magazine within eyesight.

In that moment, I just blurted it out without thinking, but as the years went by, I thought more and more about what I had said and the whole idea of a spear in general. What part of a spear garners attention? What does that attention look like? When and why is attention given to any particular area? What is the inherent value of the spear and of its individual parts?

As I moved up the ladder of Naval Special Warfare, I started to see and work behind the scenes. The manpower behind getting just one platoon ready for deployment is enormous. I saw the bigger picture of how the US fights its wars. The authorities and permissions in the way of a title (law) needed to mobilize reservist and/or guardsman teams. A mobilization is, at its basic form, converting a civilian part-time military service member into an active duty full-time military service member for at least one year, maybe more. I saw the cooperation between other government agencies in any particular theater needed to achieve our nation's goals. I started to understand the spear better. Why the shaft needs to be larger than the spearhead. Why the spearhead needs to be very well connected to the shaft. Why the metal that makes up the spearhead needs to be just right. All the parts of the spear must be their best in order to achieve its goals.

I also started reflecting on my civilian jobs and began seeing similarities to what I was experiencing back on active duty for the navy. The support behind a deputy US marshal, allowing them to focus on their charter, which is to preserve the federal justice system and enforce federal laws. When I was in the corporate setting, I saw all the people support the few executives and their initiatives. I started to reflect on my time with the CIA and—well, I'll just say that a lot of people working long hours helped us do what needed to be done.

Being the tip of the spear isn't just a position; it's also a mindset. It's a willingness to make necessary sacrifices. It's an ambition to do the best work possible—regardless of what position you hold. It's about hard work and sacrifice—so much hard work and sacrifice that it makes doing difficult work look easy. The reality is that most people who do extraordinary things are average, everyday, run-of-the-mill people who make a decision to succeed no matter how hard things get.

What I had blurted out in frustration had more significance than I had originally realized. That gut reaction revealed a deeper level of self-reflection and what it takes to get to where most of us would say we want to go but many are unwilling to follow through with. Some are not even certain where to start. What began as a negative emotion quickly turned into a desire to share my perspective with this younger generation. The more I communicated my thoughts with anyone who would listen, the more comments I received that I needed to share my ideas in a book.

So now, here we are. The book you hold in your hands is a collection of my reflections about different aspects of the spear metaphor as well as stories about my own experiences to help emphasize a particular point I'm trying to make.

What I have to share is not a new concept, but I believe it is one that is missed by many. In the KISS (in my opinion, the best band ever in the history of rock and roll) documentary, Peter Cris, the drummer, made a comment that struck me. He said, "I was tired. Tired of being on the road all the time and tired of producing record after record." To me, this is a perfect example of someone being at the tip of the spear, at the pinnacle of their industry, and yet not fully understanding what it takes to remain there. This is an example of someone who is unwilling to make the sacrifices necessary to maintain their position or role. Further on in the documentary, however, Paul Stanley (KISS's frontman) states, "This is a lifestyle; it's about the fans; it's a way of living."

Now, *he* gets it.

That understanding and ownership of what it takes to be at the tip of the spear is what keeps you there until you decide you are no longer willing to make the commitment—or until your utility is no longer wanted, needed, or useful.

The real question you must ask yourself is: Are you willing to do what it takes to get to where you want to be? More importantly, do you have what it takes to stay there?

TIP OF THE SPEAR

So, what do I mean by "tip of the spear"? This phrase has been used for generations to identify an elite group or person. Usually, the spear tip refers to the foremost forces in military operations. They are the first ones to make contact with the enemy.

Within civilian organizations, the spear tip can refer to elite groups of leaders, athletes, artists, and the like. Let's say you are an athlete, for example. In order to become elite, you need trainers, coaches, dietitians, doctors, facilities, a supporting family, and so on. There are many physically talented people out there with the drive and dedication required to succeed. However, to become elite—to become the best of the best—in most cases, you need more than what any one person has.

As an example, when I was in high school, I played on the football team. Don't get excited—it was a small school, so if you had any athletic ability at all, you made the team. I could not afford football shoes with cleats, so I played with my everyday sneakers. When I played as a wide receiver and defensive back, my footing on the field was marginal at best. At the time, I didn't care or understand how or why cleats made a big difference. However, later on, I realized I should probably get some. Sharp cuts and quick direction changes are paramount for those two positions. So, during my senior year on the football team, I found some cleats in the lost and found. They were one size too small, but I was able to get them on my feet, so I used them. My footing was much better, but boy did my feet hurt after every game.

Why am I telling you this story? To reach that elite level, it's more than just abilities. You need equipment, training, coaching, and other things around you to get there. Your mindset *combined* with everyone else's efforts makes a difference. Too many people feel like they can't reach the pinnacle because they are heads down without surrounding themselves with the right people and right equipment. If you're committed to working hard and willing to acknowledge and leverage the people and resources who can get you there, the tip of the spear is not out of reach.

Why do we refer to these elite individuals and groups as the tip of the spear? Well, the tip is usually the point of first contact with the intended target. Notably, it's also where maximum pressure can be generated by the spear.

What do I mean by that? Let me explain. Take a sharpened pencil with an eraser at the other end and place it tip down on a desk. Then, press lightly with your finger on the eraser. What do you feel in your finger? Now, turn the pencil around and place the eraser on the desk and press lightly on the pencil tip. What do you feel in your finger? Maximized energy into a smaller space increases the effect.

What is misunderstood is that being at the tip requires a level of extreme volunteerism. Holding this position is predicated by the choice to do what it takes regardless of the personal sacrifice required. It's living a lifestyle of determination, grit, and relentless effort to be the best.

It is a choice that comes with great cost.

In the private sector, this can be more easily understood by considering the difference between an hourly worker and someone who is salaried. While an employee who is on salary might make more on paper, the extra hours, commitment, and sacrifice required to accomplish the goals of the organization might very well (and often do) extend beyond what someone who is paid an hourly rate contributes. With greater authority comes greater responsibility, and this is a contribution that, at the end of the day, not everyone is willing to make. This delineation makes all the difference.

Few people recognize that only a small percentage make it to the tip—yet that has become the only place of value many see these days. What is missing is the big picture. Sacrifices are required to truly be at the tip—and to remain there. It's not a position that one can attain out of a sense of entitlement or sheer desire. There's a reason such a minority of the population occupies the tip of the spear.

For instance, consider pro athletes who still take a thousand basket shots a day or spend hours a week at the gym. Think about astronauts who are gone for months at a time in training or military leaders who sacrifice precious time and memories made with their children in order to address national security concerns. So many like the idea of being a SEAL (or other elite position) but are unwilling to count the cost and do what it takes to get there.

We are often unhappy with where we are, and yet there remains a chasm of unrealistic expectations between where we are and where we want to be.

We can see some interesting parallels when we take a look at the spear itself. Steel in its basic form is iron, which has been heated to roughly 1600°F to create what is called pig iron. The pig iron is then heated again and combined with carbon to make steel. There are many kinds of alloys, but the concept is the same: earthly elements are combined and heated to produce something of utility. This steel is then heated again, placed under pressure, and hammered to form a billet, which can be shaped through more heating, pressure, and grinding as it is worked into a point.

This process of steelmaking, and the creation of a spearhead, is a similar process of "forging," which many organizations work their people through as well. The development of elite skill sets and ideologies requires methodical training and testing, the results of which bring about the best athletes, the most successful artists, and the most powerful leaders. Anyone desiring to achieve an elite level must understand it will require rigorous development and then continual refining.

Looking at this process, it is easy to see how sailors from all walks of life and many parts of our country are combined and sifted in the "furnace" that we call Basic Underwater Demolition/SEAL training (BUD/S).

The attrition rate for candidates attempting to become Navy SEALs through BUD/S has consistently been high, reflecting the rigorous selection process. As you can likely imagine, it varies between classes but has historically ranged between 75 percent and 80 percent. This means that out of every one hundred candidates who begin BUD/S, only twenty to twenty-five successfully complete the training and advance to become SEALs. However, from the initial start to the final completion with the original BUD/S class, the success rate typically declines with attrition rising to around 85 percent to 95 percent.

To give you some background, BUD/S is structured into three primary phases.

First phase: In terms of our metaphor, we are just making steel at this point. This is when incoming recruits are heated and the slag (quitters) is removed.

The first phase focuses on physical conditioning, water competency, and teamwork exercises. Attrition rates can peak at 80 percent to 85 percent.

Put simply, the first phase is all about the suck. Long hours, lots of exercising, lots of cardio. Everyone's wet and sandy and uncomfortable most of the time. This is the phase where the notorious "Hell Week" resides. Everyone gets very little sleep for a week—if they get any at all—and people just disappear. Hell, one time after chow, my swim buddy and

I came out to our boat, and we were the only two left of our boat crew. The instructors didn't care; we were made to try to get this 350- to 400-pound rubber boat on our heads and catch up to the class. We failed.

Second phase: In our spear analogy, this is when more elements are added and impurities (more quitters) are removed.

In the second phase, the training shifts to diving techniques such as open- and closed-circuit diving as well as underwater navigation and so on—basically, the special training needed for underwater action. This phase also focuses on pool confidence exercises and open water dives. Attrition rates typically decrease somewhat during this phase but still remain significant, ranging around 20 percent to 25 percent.

Third phase: This encompasses the final refining of the steel.

The third phase integrates land warfare training, demolition exercises, continued physical conditioning, and operational planning. Attrition rates in this phase can also be notable, reaching up to 20 percent to 25 percent depending on the class.

Even after completing BUD/S, candidates must undergo additional training pipelines and evaluations. This includes Jump School, SEAL Qualification Training (SQT), and other specialized training. While attrition rates are generally lower post-BUD/S, they still exist, particularly in more specialized and demanding courses.

Becoming a Navy SEAL demands exceptional physical fitness, incredible endurance, and unwavering mental, physical, and emotional resilience. Attrition rates are influenced by a range of factors including physical conditioning, mental fortitude, teamwork, ability to perform under stress, and adherence to navy core values. The physically demanding phases of training also contribute to injury rates, further impacting attrition.

The SEAL community maintains unmatched standards, continuously evaluating candidates throughout their training. Even minor infractions or failure to meet these high standards can lead to dismissal from the program. The high attrition rates underscore the rigorous and demanding nature of SEAL training, which is designed to ensure that only the most capable candidates join one of the world's elite SOF.

What you have at the end of BUD/S is a billet of steel, which can now be shaped into a spearhead. This billet (the BUD/S graduates) then gets heated, hammered, tempered, ground, and shaped for another six months (SEAL Qualification Training). At that point, these new spearheads (SEALs) get inspected (are assigned to a command), sharpened (complete their workup), fixed to a shaft (join a task group), and sent forward to be wielded (deploy).

The tip of the spear (SEAL operators) is the point of maximum pressure. The sides of the spearhead, still lethal (senior enlisted SEAL operators with at least a few deployments under their belt), are shaped and ground to create a cutting edge. This serves to support the tip in the form of training, good examples, and mentorship, while the ridge (officer platoon OIC/SEAL operators/decision-makers) is designed to add strength to the whole of the spearhead with mission planning and overall health and welfare of the platoon. Finally, the collar (liaison, also a SEAL operator/communication with support assets) is the connection point of the spearhead to the shaft. It's part of the spearhead—where the shaft and the spearhead meet—and since it's made of the same metal, it understands what's happening at the tip and can articulate that down to the shaft. In this scenario, the shaft could be air support, transportation of the platoon, quick reaction force if things go bad, or other friendly forces in the area.

The significance of this analogy is that although not all of the spearhead is considered the *tip of the spear*, all of the spearhead has gone through the same trials and testing as the steel that makes up the tip. I think this is important to note because it is where both management and leadership reside. Their understanding of the tip should come from enduring the same process the steel at the tip has endured.

This also highlights the fact that assuming those managing or leading you haven't endured the same process as you is very narrow-minded.

There is nothing like shared experiences to help people relate to one another. If you don't believe me, why is it that when you run into someone from your same town, school, state—or country, for that matter—you are instantly friendly? I further believe that a difficult common experience compounds these emotions. Not everyone "gets us," so when we run into someone who does, we feel like we can speak freely. That being said, if you, as a manager or leader, have not been through the same trials and tribulations as those you manage, I suggest you find out what challenges your people are facing.

The truth is that there are many people and moving parts behind the scenes, in support roles, and in viable "minor" leadership roles that are vital and irreplaceable. Wherever you are, choose to find and operate from that value, being the very best you can be where you are. Embrace your position at work and your role in life. That mentality is what makes this country great—being the best YOU! In fact, that mentality is what can put you "at the tip of the spear" in your role, even if your position isn't at the tip of the spear for the organization.

People often look up to others and think they are special, but when it's all said and done, what is it that people truly admire in their role models?

The heart behind the motivation.

So often today, it seems people are looking for respect in order to be set apart or to be distinctive. Media pumps out this ideology that success is acquisition. What is lost is that feeling of responsibility to peers, family, children . . . It's a different value system altogether.

That brings up another crucial point about pursuing a place at the tip of the spear. Celebrate your heroes, but don't lose sight of celebrating yourself and of living true to your own personal philosophies. Quite possibly, your hero also did big things until it came to the point of sacrificing family, key relationships, or even their health. In the pursuit of perceived greatness, you must also safeguard against allowing those goals to come at the cost of what is most precious to you.

At the end of the day, there will always be someone better than you. SOF is a jealous mistress—at some point, she will tire of you, and you won't be her focus when someone younger and stronger comes along. In the corporate world, a customer is that same jealous mistress. If what you make or provide is no longer relevant, functional, or appropriately priced, you will lose that customer.

Being at the tip isn't a forever thing. What is forever? Relationships. Personal identity. Honor and integrity.

In the pursuit of being the best, don't disorder your priorities.

Understand that sacrifices build strength and mental toughness; at the same time, recognize that those developments are essentially what will help you foster and maintain the roles that last a lifetime (i.e., family, friendships, marriage). Find your balance and remember that sacrifice is a team effort as well. My wife will often say to me, "You will never be proud of yourself, but we are proud of you." See your journey to the tip, or at the shaft, as yours—sacred, personal, vital. Who you are in the organization, your community, and your world matters.

Do it to the best of your capacity.

RISING TO THE TOP

Too many Americans want to be something they are not. They assign little value to what or where they actually are. It's easy to see a position or title and believe that we could do better—and to perceive that where we are currently is insufficient in comparison.

In a similar vein, it's not uncommon to question the decision-makers who govern our school or workplace or romanticize the benefits of being in a different position without having a full understanding of all that comes with that level of leadership or accountability. For instance, external forces like policies, standard procedures, and legal parameters can all come into play when it comes to leadership decisions. Yet someone outside of that particular role might not recognize that. As a result, what is perceived as a misstep or inadequacy is frequently being influenced by a diverse set of circumstances that aren't being taken into account.

What is often missed is the opportunity to see the value of each individual role within an organization and why it matters to the whole. It's easy to identify another job, title, or position as more preferable. However, without understanding the unique contribution of each working part to the body and taking ownership of the sacrifice, work, or skill set involved in making the position better, many find themselves disenchanted and in a perpetual state of dissatisfaction. Subsequently, they can bring down the value of the construct they are meant to contribute to and benefit from.

I did not initially join the navy to be a SEAL. When the navy recruiter was walking the halls of my high school, he approached me and my friends and asked us what our plans were for after high school. I told him I intended to go to college for pre-med. When he asked how I was planning to pay for all that, I pulled the lint out of my pocket and shrugged my shoulders. He then proceeded to paint the picture of a path that aligned with my goal of becoming a doctor: the Naval Academy, graduation, then attending the Uniformed Services University of the Health Sciences.

With no career guidance from my parents, I was far too eager to trust anyone who could point me in the direction of becoming a doctor. So, I began to shift gears. This recruiter knew I came from modest means, so he sold me on letting the navy help me reach my goals in exchange for service to our country, all while earning a paycheck so I could still help support my mother and family financially.

Not a bad deal—or so I thought.

I took the oath of enlistment in December 1985 when I was just seventeen. At this point, I hadn't even graduated from high school. The recruiter said I needed to go to boot camp as soon as possible and then go to the Naval Academy.

Well, evidently, I'm a jackass, and while I was in boot camp, I began to learn more and more about the navy. What the recruiter had sold me was absolutely wrong. This was not the path to the Naval Academy, as I'd been told, but rather a longer route—with no guarantee I would even get in.

I was so pissed off. Here I was, stuck for the next three years, wondering what to do. Then, one day, I was reading my copy of *The Bluejacket's Manual* (the navy's bible) when I came across a section on Underwater Demolition Team (UDT)/SEALs. I knew nothing about the navy, let alone UDT/SEALs, but I knew that the reason I wanted to become a doctor was to provide a better life for my mom. So, when I saw that this UDT/SEAL program paid extra money and had a three-year commitment, I was in!

Here is the rub—there was a chasm between where I wanted to be and where I actually was. Through the

misdirection of the recruiter and my own ignorance of how I would get from A to B, I found myself in a position I didn't want to occupy. What I couldn't see at the time, however, was that I'd learn about myself through the challenges I was destined to face in those few years, and that's how I would develop a skill set I didn't know I possessed. I could have grumbled and lamented—in fact, to some, I had every right to—but I would have missed out on fully engaging in the process and learning all I could in the time I was there. Instead, I chose to find value in that temporary position and to look for opportunities to develop and grow.

About halfway through boot camp, my company marched to the swimming pool, where we met up with our sister company. A few hundred recruits were in formation when we were told this was our chance to take the screening test for the UDT/SEAL and navy diver programs. About fifty of us stepped forward to volunteer for the test, which started with a swim.

As we were getting briefed, the test administrator said we had to use the sidestroke. When he had finished and told us to enter the pool, I approached and asked him, "What is a sidestroke?" He looked at me bewildered and asked me if I knew how to do the breaststroke. I told him I did, and he said, "Do that." Then, with fifty of us in the pool at once, he said, "Go!"

Everyone took off like bats out of hell. These guys were *fast*. I was getting kicked in the face and bumped left and right until they all got in front of me. While I was swimming, I realized I was bringing up the rear and thought to myself, *I need to learn this sidestroke.*

As I kept swimming, I noticed people were already getting out of the pool. Another lap, more people out of the pool. Before long there was only me and one other guy still swimming. I was happy to no longer be getting kicked in the face but disappointed at how slow I was going.

We were dead last.

I finished and was asked to stand separate from the rest of the group. Shortly after, the other guy finished, then came over and stood next to me. We were both in parade rest—a standing position with legs slightly apart and arms behind the back, one hand over the other, considered a rest from standing at attention when in formation. I looked over at him and simply remarked, "We are slow."

My discouragement quickly turned to delighted surprise when the administrator came up to us and said we had ten minutes to change and get ready for the next event.

Not only were we the only two to pass the swim test, but we were also the only two to finish! Everyone else had quit.

Upon reflection, I am shocked at how easily people often quit—even before they ever start. I did not pass the test because I was the fastest or strongest or because I was given a head start due to my perceived "weakness." I passed because I chose to stay in my lane, do my personal best, and not worry about my skill—or lack thereof—in comparison to everyone around me.

It was mental focus that kept me in that pool and ultimately moved me forward.

From there, we continued with the screening test. The other guy didn't run fast enough for the UDT/SEAL program, but he did for the navy diver program. So, we were separated.

I alone was taken to a small room with just a chair in it and told to sit down. Two SEALs came in and started asking me why I thought I had what it took to join their ranks. They were not friendly at all. In fact, they were quite scary, honestly. Yelling and snorting. I was sure they were going to start beating me at any moment. The only thing I could say back to them was, *"I DON'T KNOW."* After what seemed like forever, they finally told me I'd better figure it out quick and instructed me to get the hell out of their office.

The rest of my time in boot camp helped me begin to find my *why*. Every morning after the screening test, the company commander would have me come up in front of the entire company, lay on my side, move my arm up and down, and make seal noises—like barking. The company commander was the active-duty sailor responsible for making us sailors—a drill sergeant for the navy's boot camp. When he'd had his fill, he would instruct me to get up and tell me loud enough so the whole company could hear him, "That's as close to being a SEAL as you're going to get." This was always met with laughter as I returned to formation.

In spite of him, I graduated boot camp and continued on to hospital corpsman "A" school. Back in my day, a sailor had to have a job or skill—called a "rate"—in the navy before going to BUD/S. A basic hospital corpsman straight out of school would be equivalent to a nurse's assistant. So now, I could empty bedpans and take someone's blood pressure.

I still didn't have orders to BUD/S, but that did not change my mind. Some of my classmates discovered that I had volunteered for the program and wished me luck. Most of them, however, felt the need to warn me, "It's too hard. You won't make it."

One week before "A" school graduation, I received my orders to BUD/S. In December 1986, I classed up with Class 143, alongside about 120 or so fellow students.

Once again, I started running into classmates who, for some reason, felt compelled to tell me, "You're not going to make it." As training went on and the self-appointed you-don't-have-what-it-takes authorities themselves quit, I found myself becoming increasingly motivated. As more and more of my classmates gave up, it pushed me even harder.

I remember an evolution during "Hell Week" called "Around the World." This consisted of very long inflatable boat small (IBS) paddles, very long land portage with the IBS on our heads, and us being wet and cold for hours. Oh, and it was a race—one that took hours to complete.

Whether this was by design or because our class was really that slow, I'm not sure, but the instructors decided to make us do it again. My class manned our boats, and we started running to the bay side of the base to insert our boats to start the race. It was dark outside, the middle of February, and *cold*. I was in the center of the boat crew on the left side with one guy in front of me. We started down the ramp, and I'll never forget the look on this guy's face once his ankles hit the frigid water. It was a look of terror that quickly turned into an expression of determination to get warm come hell or high water. When you quit during "Hell Week," the instructors give you a warm blanket and a cup of cocoa. Too funny. Presumably lured by the promise of warmth, he dropped his part of the boat and quit on the spot. Of course, we tried to talk him out of it—I think probably because we needed the extra help and wanted to win the race . . . not so much to keep him around—but there was no changing his mind.

What was even more memorable was seeing him the following week in the chow hall. He was embarrassed, sad, just depleted of any self-worth. I didn't care or even fault him. I knew how much it sucked. I think he was feeling that way because now he had to face the people most important to him as a failure. *Get over it.* At least he tried.

I graduated with the class I started with—Class 143.

So, what drove me? You see, everyone who'd said that I wouldn't make it or that I didn't have what it took had no idea what was required to make it through. They themselves hadn't made it or even truly attempted to in most cases. The two guys who actually did know what it took because they were already SEALs (the guys back in boot camp who I thought were going to kill me) never said I wouldn't make it—they told me to figure it out. So I did.

My "why" was in proving to everyone who said I couldn't, shouldn't, or wouldn't make it *wrong*. I alone determine my future. Period.

I think I've made my point.

Prior to graduation, we had the opportunity to mail out invitations to anyone we wanted. I sent one to each individual who had said I wouldn't make it. I hadn't been able to argue with them back when they had doubted me because, at that time, I honestly didn't know myself whether I could do it. But when I did, you bet your ass that I got their addresses and sent them all invites.

Oddly, none of them showed up!

After BUD/S graduation, at my first opportunity to go back home, I visited that recruiter who had led me astray. As soon as I walked into his office, he jumped out of his chair, shuddering, and said, "I didn't know you wanted to be a SEAL!"

"I didn't," I responded.

He knew he'd done me dirty, that the Naval Academy required an officer recruiter to run the process to help get me an appointment to the academy, not an enlisted recruiter like he was who just sent me to boot camp. He also knew that I knew he was afraid and thought that I was there to settle a score. However, I left it at that. I think he was grateful I didn't pay him back.

Put simply, I went back to see this recruiter not to settle a score but to let him know I'd made the best out of the cards I was dealt. His misdirection had actually ended up taking me to places he couldn't have imagined.

Sometimes what looks like a setback, whether self- or others-inflicted, can be the catalyst for something better than what we could have planned.

Although I was no closer to being a doctor, I was sending more money home for the family and performing a critical role for my mom. In that sense, I was pursuing my goals—albeit in a different way than I had imagined.

When I went back to active duty in 2009, I was frequently asked to speak with young adults considering BUD/S. Not once did I ever tell any of them they couldn't, shouldn't, or wouldn't make it through. Regardless of their background, fitness level, or gender, I told them it is a choice— their choice. If they wanted to join our ranks and live this lifestyle, the work would never end, but if they wanted it, the choice was theirs.

If you want it, only you can figure out what you need to do to get it.

YOU ARE MORE THAN JUST YOURSELF

When I first classed up for BUD/S, I was met with other students telling me I was not going to make it through because I was a hospital corpsman (navy medic), I was eighteen (going on nineteen) years old, and historically, corpsmen and teenagers quit this program. *Blah, blah, blah.* As you've probably picked up on by now, those comments just motivated the shit out of me to prove those naysayers wrong. I was now representing all the teenagers and hospital corpsmen in the world whether they knew or not, like the tip of the spear that represents the whole of the spear.

What's the message here? Find motivation outside of yourself. You are greater than the sum of your parts. If you behave poorly or if you're quick to give up, you are not just letting yourself down. You represent your parents, siblings, friends, school, town, team, company, service, state, and country . . . The list goes on and on. Think of all the people who will find joy in your success. If you only had to answer to yourself, you might be too quick to give up—never realizing your full potential. Never seeing what others see in you. If the tip of a spear is not sharp enough or strong enough to penetrate its target, the whole of the spear has failed.

I once asked a good friend of mine, a fellow SEAL, "When do we stop having to represent?" I had an idea of what he was going to say. Sure enough, he answered, "Never," and he was right. If I ever went to the dark side and for some reason got caught by the law, the headlines would read, "Retired Navy SEAL commander arrested for ABC," or "Ex-CIA operative arrested for XYZ," or "Navy SEAL from Washington state caught doing 456 . . ." What it won't say is, "Rodney Magallan arrested for 123." Who the hell is Rodney Magallan? Nobody. But *who I represent*—now *that* is what matters, and that is why we can never stop representing. And that's OK. Remember, a thousand "atta boys" are erased by one "oh shit."

WHY IT MATTERS

A lot of people love to talk about being the best or admire those considered to be at the "top." However, most have very little understanding of what it actually takes to get there, let alone the sacrifice and mentality required to maintain that position.

Over the years, people have said to me, "I wanted to be in the military," or, "Yeah, I thought of trying out for the SEAL program." What I think they are trying to say is, "That is so inspiring, and it looks so great." What I hear, however, is, "I chose not to," or "Yeah, I could have done that," as though we are the same. To be honest, it minimizes the effort and sacrifice I made by implying that just anyone can be at the top. The truth is that just thinking about choosing a different lifestyle is a great deal different from actually making the choice to give up everything to get there.

Being part of an elite group seems appealing from the outside looking in, but more often than not, people will instead take what is immediately in front of them—something more familiar or seemingly attainable—and miss the opportunity to achieve something higher for themselves. Or they step back when it appears they might have to give up more of themselves, their resources of time and output, than they are willing to commit.

Regardless of intention, what is being communicated to someone who has chosen to step into that elite position is that just *anyone* can do it. This diminishes the effort the elite person put in. It also shows that the person trying to relate wasn't willing to put in the effort to even see if it was possible for them to become elite. What is most likely intended as a compliment or a point of connectivity actually diminishes the value of the sacrifice given in order to achieve that position or role.

There's an important lesson here. While people at the tip can sometimes come across as short or rude, the truth is that we know what it takes.

It is what it is. No excuses. No shrinking back. We faced the improbable and told ourselves there was no other option. We don't care much about what you *thought* about doing; we care about what you *actually* do—and how well you do it. Period.

We live by a can-do attitude, which, to be honest, never changes, regardless of the passage of time or the environments we inhabit. That mentality and personal positioning is *who* we are, wherever we are, regardless of the role. It's not something we turn on and off based on whether we're in a position where we are "seen." It's a core value that does not ebb and flow based on opportunity or recognition. Regardless of the space in which we operate, we work and give from the perspective that it's all or nothing in spite of perceived resources or current external influences.

Becoming the best at anything requires a mindset and drive to get you into that space. Once you have achieved that position, you need that same mindset and drive to perform at a level that allows you to stay in said space. Now, when I talk about position in this context, I don't necessarily mean job title. I am talking about doing what you do better than most. There are many car companies, but few hold that elite position in the industry demanding hundreds of thousands of dollars more than the competition.

It is this thought process that gets one to the tip—a mental toughness that I truly believe anyone can attain if they put their mind and effort into it.

The question is: How important is it to you? Do you want it bad enough to make it your priority? To refuse to take *no* for an answer? Do you have what it takes? More critically, if you don't have what it takes, are you willing to find out *how* to bridge that gap to get to where you say you want to be?

So many idealize the idea of being a strategic instrument of war or of climbing the ladder of success, but very few are willing to be humbled, challenged, or brought to their perceived limits of capability in order to be sharpened. When it all comes down to it, regardless of where we come from or what tools we think we have, the bottom line is individual choice.

Always.

What are your personal obstacles to committing to "go"? Do you just want bragging rights, a pretty headline, or an inspiring Instagram feed? Or are you willing to face the mountain head-on and take ownership of the process?

In today's culture, there is an emphasis on instant gratification, and it can often seem as though some are just charmed, while others simply are not. People may think that someone has gotten to their position at the tip of the spear by chance, and they may falsely believe they can skyrocket to elite status if they get a lucky break. The truth, however, is that to get to the pinnacle of our craft or career, sacrifices must be made, goals must be clearly defined, and growth (sometimes painful) must be experienced. Bottom line? You gotta get dirty and get out of your own way.

Some of the obstacles I have noticed in myself and others over the years include failing to understand the full value of my own individual role, neglecting to take a look at the organization as a whole, and dealing with the fear of doing my best and possibly still failing. Success is not a straight shot, nor does it come without trial and error, humility, and sometimes sheer grit.

True failure, however, is when you stop trying altogether and choose not to take those learning experiences to the next effort or level.

So often, people blame others for their position or potential. Factors like upbringing and family of origin, relationships, culture, or financial accessibility are often elevated above their own shortfalls or weaknesses. It can be easy to inventory what we have or have not been given when we compare ourselves to those around us. The problem is that when we focus on ourselves instead of setting our sights on the goal itself, we set ourselves up for failure before we even begin. While external influences can have a real effect on our lives, we alone carry within ourselves the potential to persevere through personal setbacks and grow as individuals.

Personally, I failed at becoming a doctor. Not because I couldn't but because I stopped trying. That failure, though, does not prevent me from excelling somewhere else. Learning, fighting, growing, failing, succeeding—these are all part of the journey, no one greater or of less value when filtered through a big picture, long-game perspective.

The takeaway here is this: we are all dealt a certain hand in life. Regardless of our circumstances, we have to take the initiative to relentlessly pursue our goals if we want to be the best of the best. Making excuses, blaming others, or getting impatient for the end result before you've put the work in isn't going to get you there. It is so important to stop looking for others to give us a break, to tear down barriers, or to offer us an open door to areas we have not yet created the opportunity to access ourselves.

How does leadership play into this? It captures everything we've talked about and even goes a step further. A leader is someone who also inspires those around them to do what they didn't think they could or what they wouldn't dare to attempt if left to their own devices. True leaders move, grow, and develop as they empower those around them to do the same. A leader sees obstacles and barriers as opportunities to make themselves and others better, stronger, faster, and more aware.

OPPORTUNITIES

We live in the freest country in the world. Now, I didn't say the *easiest* country but the freest. Free to pursue anything that has been done before or blaze the way for something totally new.

If it is doable, why not you?

When my grandfather left his homeland of Mexico, he came to the United States for safety and to take advantage of fresh opportunities. He wasn't asking for handouts; he just wanted to provide an honest day's work in order to take care of his family. He and his family worked in the fields as migrant laborers, and they all became US citizens or at least resident aliens (green card holders).

Like the rest of my family, I also worked in the fields when I was young. There is nothing wrong with working in the fields. In fact, picking fruit is probably as close as you can physically get to the concept of "effort equals reward." How much we brought in, not the hours we worked, was how we were paid. Now, I was not very good at picking fruit or cutting asparagus. I did learn to respect the folks that are willing to work in this capacity, but . . . f**k that shit. I decided, *I'm going to college.*

Growing up, those experiences and the example set by those around me taught me the value of putting family first. I saw my friends' parents, my teachers, and the folks who ran local businesses prioritizing hard work so they could give their kids, and themselves, a better life— one that reflected core values and a deep commitment to putting their hand (and mind) to something. Not that things were ever easy, but as an adult, I still believe, and have proven to myself, that when I choose a never-say-die, just-do-it attitude, the only limitations in my way are by my own making.

We live in a microwave society; we tend to value success but not the time, commitment, and effort required to achieve it. Life doesn't just give—it takes. It takes in the form of effort. When did we as a society start believing that we are incapable? I think that this generation has been given a great deal with not as much responsibility, which has inadvertently stunted their capacity to fully recognize their personal potential—or to find value or satisfaction in working hard.

Sometimes I look at my own kids, and while I always wanted to provide for them, I now see that they haven't ever truly experienced lack. Struggle is not necessarily bad; it creates a hunger, builds strength, and reveals to us our own tenacity and capacity. In today's culture, however, struggle or lack is seen as a problem to be covered rather than an opportunity to grow.

Blessings without accountability create weakness.

Working hard to make ends meet, budgeting, starting at the bottom, and being hungry for more is what actually builds the grit and life skills that help to move us toward the tip.

To reiterate, struggle isn't bad. It's all about choosing to shift your perspective. When looking at a spearhead that has just been thrust into something hard, you will find small deformities. These take away from the overall effectiveness of the spearhead but are a natural occurrence. In order to return the spearhead, let alone the tip, back to max effectiveness, we need to hone the edges with something harder than the steel that makes up the spearhead, taking little bits of steel away until we reach our desired shape and sharpness. That honing happens through struggle.

Accept it, learn from it, and grow through it.

PURPOSE

The design and purpose of the tip of the spear is to penetrate—to create chaos or to bring a change in power or direction. It is created to be the business end of the spear as a whole.

When you think about the tip of an arrow and the tip of a bullet, you might recognize there are quite a few similarities. In some ways, these have the same purpose as a spearhead. But why do we say *tip of the spear* and not tip of the arrow or bullet?

I believe the reason is because it is implied that we intend to preserve the spear. We don't plan on losing it. An arrow or a bullet is used once and seldom retrieved, whereas the spear is expected to be used over and over again. The spear can be thrown, but that is not the best use of it.

Now, let's chat a bit about the cutting edge of the spearhead.

As we've briefly discussed, to sharpen the spearhead, it takes grinding, usually with something that is harder than the steel that is being sharpened. Grinding away some of the steel is necessary to reach the desired degree of sharpness. Please understand that—and this is super important to note—not all of the original steel from the cutting edge or tip of the spear is going to survive this grind. Few people make it into the most elite groups, and even fewer will actually stay long enough to retire at the highest level. It is only natural—in order to sharpen something, you need to remove something.

This concept of grinding away can represent itself in various forms within an organization. An individual may decide they no longer want to pursue that lifestyle or operate at that level of commitment. Alternatively, the falling away can come as a result of someone's physical or mental health getting worn down or diminished. Not everyone is designed or motivated to maintain a position of leadership or a lifestyle of extreme sacrifice indefinitely. The question is: Are you truly not designed for this? Or are you simply unwilling to step into what it takes emotionally, physically, mentally, and relationally in order to achieve and maintain that position?

As a civilian in the early 2000s, I was working overseas with a unit that was hunting high-value targets (HVT). The senior enlisted in charge of the unit found out that I had formerly been an enlisted SEAL. He was interested in why I had left active duty in my prime because he was losing many of his experienced guys around the same time I had left—around the fourteen-year mark—and was looking for a solution to his problem. I asked him to give me a couple of days to think about it before I gave him my opinion. (Of course, I reminded him that "opinions are like assholes; we all have one, and they all stink.") It didn't take me long to identify the "why," and I realized that finding a solution would be difficult if one existed at all.

I went back and shared that the reason I believed this group was losing its more experienced guys was simple: their priorities shifted. The men were now in their thirties, probably married, and likely to have at least one child, if not more. (Honestly, that's why I left active duty at that time in my life.) I also pointed out that this lifestyle has a "best-used-by" date. Once we have passed that date, we are essentially just in the way.

Now, to all of you still crushing it in your thirties, forties, and so on, don't misunderstand me here. I'm talking about being a door-kicker in this specific organization. As we move into our late thirties and early forties, this lifestyle starts to get old. I could go on and on about the toll on our bodies and relationships, but that will be for another time.

Let's just say my marriage has survived to retirement, my best-used-by date has passed, and I'm in my forties and still need to provide for my wife and kids. Personally, I left for a job that still gave me satisfaction (as a deputy US marshal), and I could now provide well for the family into my late fifties.

What I recommended wasn't much help to this particular group, but I did suggest identifying those guys getting ready to launch and transition them into professional support roles the unit utilizes now, like lawyers, doctors, or engineers, which would allow them to continue contributing their wisdom and experience while providing for their family well into their sixties or seventies. This strategy also keeps the experience in-house and is a small gesture to give back to those from whom we have asked so much.

I shared that it was the hardest decision of my life leaving a job that I was pretty damn good at. But, at the end of the day, "Rodney the Operator" was out-voted by "Rodney the Dad" and "Rodney the Husband" two to one.

We don't see it when we are nineteen or twenty, single with only ourselves, our gear, and our teammates to think about. But eventually, we all evolve into something greater than the sum of our parts. Being a dad and a husband is no small task. To be the best at those roles also takes sacrifices that often include stepping away from things that no longer serve us or that we don't serve with our whole selves anymore.

Returning to our analogy, I would also like to point out that this grinding is what people at the cutting edge or at the tip usually experience. The intense sharpening of the spearhead is how the majority of elite groups/people/positions are trained and are expected to perform and develop—both within the military and in civilian jobs. Blood, sweat, and tears are expended in preparation to be used at a high capacity, only occasionally and for a short period of time. I knew I couldn't keep kicking down doors until my body gave out. Founders of start-up companies eventually take a step back. Athletes retire or become coaches.

The feathers or artwork (praise or positive attention) that often decorate the shaft rarely adorn the spearhead, and the tip even less so. The attention given to the tip of the spear is predominantly brought on by, or through, something harder than the steel. Often, that attentiveness to its viability (sharpening) is given only when it's being prepared to be used. Frankly, there is no room at the tip for feathers or artwork, as it is largely utilitarian.

I want to remind you that the sharpening process takes away, refines, and does not add. If one were to choose to make the tip pretty, would you be so quick to thrust it into harm's way? Absolutely not. Subsequently, for as long as you intend to remain at the tip, expect that this sharpening will be the primary form of treatment you will experience, and establish in your mind that that's OK.

For those who operate at the shaft, be proud of your feathers and artwork, but don't for a second compare yourself to the spearhead, let alone the tip. The shaft has different roles, is prepared for use in different ways, and is a lot more easily approached compared with something designed to cut and destroy. The shaft is also more visible compared to the spearhead, and in many ways, the responsibility falls differently.

The main reason I warn against comparing yourself to someone else, however, is to save your pride. Be you! Don't be like *this* or like *them*. Know your role and do it to the best of your ability. Find your vision and pursue it relentlessly. Being authentically you and taking ownership of your position (as well as recognizing its value) is a mindset, and it's separate from having long-term goals. You can aspire to grow and reach toward a different position, but don't neglect your current value or give anything less than your best in the process of getting to where you ultimately want to be. When you come to terms with who you are, you'll be much happier, less stressed, and more effective to the organization (and yourself!) as a whole.

OVERCOMING TRAUMA

Growing up, there were a lot of situations that I could choose to categorize as lack or "trauma." Where I came from, being disciplined with violence was the norm, and not everyone chose the straight and narrow, if you know what I mean. It was not uncommon for me to endure beatings and verbal abuse, and without going into too much detail, the household I grew up in was not necessarily a loving or safe one. As a result, I knew from an early age that if I wanted to do something, I had to do it myself.

That being said, here is the truth—we can either sink or swim. I don't have any more talents or strengths than the next guy, but what I do have is the work ethic and mentality to turn what could potentially hold me back into stepping stones for building something different.

A long time ago, my family was on welfare. In the state of Washington, back in the day, welfare had a program where able-bodied youngsters could work, and the state would pay a portion of the wages.

When I was fourteen, my mom told me I had gotten a job working as a janitor's assistant. I didn't ask for the job, I didn't apply for it, but one day, I had a job, and after school, I needed to go help the janitor. I never saw a paycheck while I worked there, but I know I have been paying taxes since I was fourteen, so I must have been getting paid. My mom got the money. I didn't complain because we had a roof over our heads and food in our bellies. I would go to school, attend practice for whatever sport was in season (in secret because my mom didn't believe in sports and saw it as a waste of time), then head down to the elementary school to start cleaning.

The gentleman I worked for was fair, and he didn't treat me like a kid. One day, he threw me the keys to this old truck and told me to move it to the back of the school. Well, I'm showing my age here, but the truck had what they called a "three on the tree" type shifter. Half of you are probably wondering what a shifter is, let alone a three on the tree type shifter. I'll describe it as best I can. Foot pedal clutch. Lever on the right side of the steering column. The lever would go up and down with a little front-to-back action to select the gear you wanted.

Did I mention there were no numbers, letters, or any indicators letting me know what gear I was in? I was familiar with a clutch, having helped my friends on their farms drive tractors. Push in the clutch. *Check.* Turn the key. *Check.* Find first gear. *No check.* First gear! *No check.* Any gear? *Check.* The only gear I could manage to move the truck with was reverse. So, I moved that truck to the back of the school.

In reverse.

What I didn't realize was that the janitor was watching me the whole time. Once I turned the truck off, he came over and asked me if I had ever driven this kind of truck before. When I said no, he asked me why I hadn't told him. I replied, "I'm only fourteen. I thought you knew and wanted me to move the truck anyway." He laughed and tasked me with more chores until my time was up for the day.

To be clear, this man wasn't judging me. He had things to do and probably thought I knew how to drive. And I knew I didn't need to fear telling him I had never driven a truck before. I wasn't going to disappoint him. He wanted to teach me—that's all.

Even though I saw no dollar amount for my efforts because the funds went directly to my mother, I was content in the support roles I was given. Helping the janitor do the best he could for the school, no matter how small our town was, and helping my mother provide food and shelter for our family was a position in the shaft I was happy to possess at the time.

I worked at the school on weekends as well. One Saturday, the janitor tasked me with cleaning the second-floor windows inside and out. Now, this was an older building, and I think at one time it was the town's high school—just to give you a visual. It took me all day to clean those windows. When I finished, I was going to put things away when the janitor came up to me with an excited air and said, "Come with me!" I immediately thought I had done something wrong.

He led me to the front of the building and asked me to look up at the windows.

I inspected them for a minute and then asked him, "What's wrong? Did I break something?"

He glanced at me and replied, "Nothing is wrong. Those windows look great. I want you to see what a good job you did. It's the little things that impact us the most."

That feeling of a job well done is addictive. I thank him for teaching me that.

While some might assume that working through my childhood and being responsible for helping meet our family's needs was hard, maybe even unfair or traumatic, it was part of what developed my can-do mindset and solidified an internalized value in working hard and providing well. Such values have served me so very well in this life.

Anyone can earn. Anyone can hustle. It's why so many people flock to the United States. Remove that trauma mindset and stop focusing on what "almost" happened—or didn't happen—for you. Set your eyes on where you are headed and use the life lessons you have been given to sharpen you, to renew your thinking, and to motivate your next moves.

Our body is actually designed to heal itself. We get a cut, we heal, we scar. The brain sets up a system to address the injury, and subsequently, the skin becomes tougher. Similarly, our minds can be trained to do the same with emotional, relational, and situational wounds or discrepancies. The mind will adjust to *how you frame a situation*.

Why do we deny our mind the opportunity to heal naturally? Making lemonade out of lemons is not just a pie-in-the-sky idea—we are hardwired to effectively channel negative energy and situations into growth opportunities. Even nature speaks to the value of vision and tenacity. The smallest seed works its way out of the dirt to become a tree, and a flower in the concrete breaks through to reach toward the sun. You *can* grow through where you've been.

Don't give your past too much power—use it to power up!

In order to understand what all it entails to become the tip of the spear, one must also take into account the contribution of the shaft and even of the very hand itself that wields the weapon. The responsibility of being at the pinnacle of one's career or life choices must also come with the comprehension of the inherent value each contributor brings to any organization or even family. For many of us, there tends to be a hierarchy, sometimes even a discrediting of those positions or skill sets that are considered to be of less importance. In order for functionality to operate at its greatest capacity, however, no one part can be—or even be perceived as—lesser or greater than the other.

> "I was raised to treat the janitor with the same
> respect as the CEO." —Tom Hardy

While most of us would agree with this sentiment in ideal, it is a little more difficult to internalize and put into practice, especially when we find ourselves in the position of the shaft, in the shadow of the tip. It is easy to see value in position or status, but what is so often missed is the contribution of each individual part to the functionality of the whole. At the end of the day, each position is dependent on the viability of the others in order to achieve success.

Considering a spear's application to any organization, let's look at some of the dynamics of the weapon itself. The shaft is usually not made from the same steel but has similar elements in its creation, like iron. The shaft is the main body of the spear. Frankly, without a shaft, the spearhead is just steel looking for something to do.

So why is the tip revered but often simultaneously shied away from? And what does any of this mean to you? It is my goal to lead you down a path of self-discovery that will hopefully enlighten, inspire, and propel you to greater heights, wherever you might find yourself.

SOLO

A spear tip without the rest of the spear.

A spear tip, similar to arrowheads that can be found all over the southwest United States, are artifacts that people collect and put on the shelf to look at. They are often perceived as having passed their utility. A spearhead without the rest of the spear ends up being just that—a relic.

One can also make the comparison to bullets from the Civil War that are found on the East Coast. All these pieces of lead that, back in the day, were mostly used once and then abandoned are now relics to be collected—never to destroy or create chaos again.

A spearhead, however, is not tied to any one shaft. In fact, it can be fixed to other shafts as demands change. These shafts could be two different companies, organizations, or government agencies. One example of this would be people transitioning from active-duty military to, say, law enforcement or a group of people starting their own business after working together at a larger company.

I will warn you that not all spearheads are created equal. Weak steel looks very similar to ideal steel but can be quite different in how it performs. How do you know if your steel falls short? Unfortunately, it takes putting it to the test to be confident in its viability. Possible areas of weakness include the steel being unable to hold a cutting edge, bending easily, or chipping or breaking upon first use. Although it may look like a resilient spearhead, it is useless if it cannot perform the job properly.

More often than not, if folks attach this new, weaker spearhead to a different shaft, they will only realize it is not made of what they had hoped for after first contact. Likewise, when ill-equipped or unproven people (weak "steel") lie, hide, or fake what their true capabilities are, the organization as a whole is weakened. In order to be an effective unit, employees must be honest, fair, and truthful (with themselves and their team) so that the "spear" operates as it's designed to.

Remember, leaders at the top want to put the right people in the right places. Knowing who you truly are enables them to place you in the best position for not only the success of your peers but for you!

Contrary to the belief of many, it is not disgraceful to identify your shortcomings. In fact, such transparency is often actually preferred because now you can do something about them! Training and supplemental teams can strengthen areas of weakness to address vulnerability in the spear's (team's) performance. So, have the courage to ask questions, find a mentor, and be transparent about who you are and what you can contribute. (Humility and courage are symbiotic.)

Training programs, seminars, and webinars are all vital components to your personal and professional growth and development. It takes strength and wisdom to recognize that we all have areas where we can become stronger, and developmental resources, if we are open to them, are endless. Take advantage of them!

Don't forget—no organization wants anyone to suck at his or her job, and most decision-makers prefer honesty over perfection. The idea that we "have to know everything" is often self-imposed. Even when we seemingly miss out on an opportunity, it usually results in a new door opening to where we fit best.

Think of your position as a piece of the puzzle—know what your role is and be OK with it. Maybe you are needed where you are to make the team the strongest it can be. If that position is in the shaft, perhaps that's where you belong—and you can still maintain a tip of the spear mindset and maintain that high level of performance within your role.

Bottom line: trust the process!

When I made the decision to leave active duty (my SEAL buddies would call it quitting), I had to go through the Marshal Service hiring process. Forms needed to be filled out, a background check had to be done, a physical fitness test was performed, and a medical exam was required. There were no issues—or so I thought. Wouldn't you know it, I almost did not qualify due to a medical condition.

There I was getting a physical, and we came to the eye exam. The results: 20/15 left eye, 20/15 right eye. Pretty good. Then, this doctor handed me a pair of funky glasses, opened a book with a fly in the middle, and asked me to pinch the wings. I pressed my fingers upon the page and pinched them together. The doc closed the book and asked for his glasses back. Then, he looked at me and said I'd failed the medical exam.

"Due to what?" I asked, taken aback.

He told me I had no depth perception. Incredulous, I asked him what his definition of depth perception was.

"Depth perception is the ability to judge how far away something is," he responded.

I reached out and touched him on the nose, asking him, "Like that?"

He pulled back, a little embarrassed, and reiterated that I had failed the test.

Now, what was going through my mind at this point was, *You've got to be shitting me.* Thirteen years as a SEAL; over six hundred free-fall jumps; free-fall jumpmaster; sniper; operator of multiple vehicles next to other vehicles going really fast; hell of a shot; apprentice instructor in Kali and Thai boxing; and much, much more. But I don't have depth perception?

Now, I'm not bragging. I'm just trying to make sense of this stupid ass test that said I didn't have what it takes to be a deputy US marshal. I calmed myself down, took his paperwork, went home, and started researching depth perception exams. When I had enough information, I scheduled another physical exam, as I had lost the paperwork from the previous one. Lo and behold, I passed the physical with flying colors.

Perhaps some of you out there may be thinking that I was a hypocrite or being deceitful, but that goes against my character and everything I've said so far. Listen, I had no doubt in my mind that I would be an asset to the Marshal Service. (In fact, if I had not struggled with one of the law exams, I would have been the honor graduate. I know this only because one of my class proctors told me as much, as he had a side bet with some of the other academy instructors.) When I speak of lying or faking, I am talking about your abilities. I was not hiding or faking; in fact, I wanted to show the Marshal Service what I could do.

Not tell them—show them.

And that's what I encourage you to do. Identifying shortfalls is always better than hiding them. Living unauthentically quickly turns into a full-time job of lying about what you can do and faking your way through the day-to-day while constantly being anxious that someone will find out how overmatched you truly are. This is unnecessary stress, not just to the person hiding but to the organization as well. Be honest and get better or settle into your sweet spot and thrive. When we are fully thriving, we are operating at our greatest potential and living a reduced-stress life at work and beyond.

Toward the end of my time in the navy, when I held the rank of commander, I was the commanding officer of a Navy Operational Support Center (NOSC). We were charged with the administrative care, feeding, and mobilization readiness of the reserve sailors attached to the command. Although reserve sailors are responsible for maintaining the same standards as an active-duty sailor, as they may be called to active duty, many have difficulty understanding the commitment they signed up for.

One weekend, I addressed my three-hundred-plus sailors: "I will help you achieve the rank where you feel most comfortable."

It was quiet for a moment, and then one of the sailors raised his hand and asked me, "Does that mean you will bust us down in rank too?"

I paused, walked closer to the sailor, smiled at him, and said, "If that is where you feel the most comfortable."

Now, busting someone down in rank is no easy task. But I am willing to take that approach if necessary because, as I explained to my sailors, the American people believe—no, *expect*—our military to be the best in the world. How would you like to explain to your hometown, family, or grandparents that you made a commitment to our country, took a highly sought-after position in the service, and enjoyed their taxes in the form of compensation, but you don't want to live up to their expectations? Laws are constantly passed in support of our veterans—all of America is asking of you is to do what you said you would.

DO YOUR JOB.

Unfortunately, poor performance or downright insubordination is often tolerated. This does nothing for the organization and even less for the person who is falling short of expectations. I can't tell you how many times my peers have chosen to manage substandard soldiers and performance by merely sweeping things under the rug.

Now, don't get me wrong—Lord knows there was also a time when I took care of my teammates following that philosophy. What I grew to understand, though, was that while covering up for consistently poor performance was the easiest path for me, it did nothing to benefit the person falling short (or the group as a whole for that matter). Leading that way often placed me, as the decision-maker, in a tight spot. More importantly, it significantly damaged morale among the ranks.

Conversely, if you yourself are in a position where you are on the receiving end of correction, be humble. You should not only accept responsibility for your own development but also recognize that it is your perceived value to the organization or team that prompts those in leadership to redirect you. It's important to embrace the truth that our contribution matters to the whole and that our corporate achievement also fosters personal success.

Holding people accountable for their commitment or correcting poor behavior/performance is the hard road that needs to be traveled in order to achieve long-term success. It is what I committed to when I accepted a position of responsibility. (Although, I acknowledge that not every good leader is in a position of responsibility, and not everyone in a position of responsibility is a good leader.) I was enlisted for sixteen years before becoming an officer, and it gave me the foundation and experience to learn a great deal about the weight of leadership.

That being said, here are a few key values that helped me—and that can help you—transition effectively to a leadership position:

1. Always do your personal best to set the expectation.
2. Be willing to change the way you train/teach based on the team.
3. Think outside the box.
4. Don't ask someone to do what you wouldn't do.
5. Take advantage of opportunities, not people.

At the end of the day, success comes when every person, regardless of position, respects and understands the role they play and the value they offer—as well as that of those they work alongside—and how that affects the overall health and goals of the organization.

IN DUE SEASON

I'll never forget where I was on 9/11. I was a deputy US marshal at the time. My partner and I were on our way to Arizona to pick up a prisoner and bring him back to Texas. While waiting for our flight transfer at William P. Hobby Airport, we noticed people crowding around the television sets throughout the terminal. We made our way to one of them and started watching just in time to see the second plane hit the tower. I turned to my partner and told her, "We are going to war."

The airport was quickly shut down, and we stepped in to help evacuate the terminals. People were angry their flights had been canceled (I know, right?!) The United States had just been attacked on our own soil, and yet many just couldn't comprehend the gravity of what had happened.

We made our way to the Houston office, borrowed a car, and drove back to our home office in Corpus Christi. As soon as I had the opportunity, I called the SEAL Team I was attached to as a reservist and asked, "When are you going to activate me?" I was still in the reserves at the time, meaning that to transition from a civilian part-time sailor, I needed some kind of orders to active duty or full-time sailor status.

The response from the operations department was, "We are not activating anyone yet, but you can reenlist."

I didn't know enough about the reserves then, and I thought if I reenlisted, I would have to give up my job as a deputy US marshal. At this point, I had been a reservist for just over one year. I had not educated myself on what was in the realm of possibilities as a reservist to serve on active duty without giving up my civilian job, so I thought if I reenlisted, I'd be screwed. Later, as I learned more about the reserves, I found out that a reservist can reenlist for up to five years during a time of war and still come back to their civilian jobs. Oh well.

From there, I called a US Marine unit and told them, "I'm a navy corpsman. I am an 18D [Army Special Forces] trained medic. Will you activate me since we are going to war?"

The Marine's response was the same as SEAL Team 4's: "We are not activating anyone, but you can reenlist."

What I came to learn later in my career as a SEAL officer primarily managing reservists was that you need authorities and permissions in the form of a title (law) to activate them.

Bummed out, I waited for a call. Finally, I received one.

The conversation went something like this: "Your name was passed on to us. Would you be interested in interviewing with our organization?"

I asked them just one question: "Do I get to go to Afghanistan?"

There was a long pause before he answered with a firm, "Yes." Without hesitation, I told him to send me the plane tickets. I had no idea who I was talking to, what organization it was, or what I would be doing, but I knew I'd be closer to the fight, and at the time, that was where I needed to be.

When I told my wife what I had done, she looked at me and said, "You do what you need to do." I interviewed and was hired a few months later. In a week's time, I was onboarded, all the while knocking out requirements before heading downrange for my first deployment as a GRS protective agent for the CIA.

Here is the crux. Had I not already been forged in the crucible of the SEAL Teams, I would not have been able to be so quickly onboarded. More importantly, I would not have been useful downrange. What you are working on today, where you are being developed and stretched, is not always necessarily for your current position. A commitment to living a life of intentionality is what prepares you for opportunities before they even present themselves.

THE SPEAR SHAFT

Some might argue that a spear shaft without a spearhead has more utility. It still has reach. It can move a boat in shallow water. You can play stickball with it. It can be used as support when you're hiking the backcountry. Ultimately, in the right hands, it can still be used as a weapon—with or without a spearhead. Don't get me wrong—we need people willing to sacrifice and work hard to be the tip of the spear, but we also need people willing to work hard and allow sacrifice to be a way of life to maintain their position on the shaft.

It's extremely important for people to understand what it takes to be elite and to understand that elite groups and individuals are more effective when whoever supports them comprehends why *their* support matters—and then strives to be the best at that until they are no longer in that support role. No one gets to the tip or maintains a position there without help from the shaft.

The spear shaft can include myriad disciplines. Sticking with the military model, an example would be your legal, logistical, and administrative support. (Authorities and permissions from the Constitution supporting our missions and the families supporting us back home so we can focus on the job at hand could fall in the spear shaft too.)

Regarding the difference between the wood and metal used in creating a spear, I found that the common element necessary for both to thrive is iron. Iron ore is melted at 1600°F in order to remove the impurities. Then, it is processed further by adding carbon to finally become workable steel. Similarly, that very same iron element in the soil is vital to the growth and healthy development of plants and trees. It's a fine balance yet still a common element that both steel and wood share.

The inference here is that the people who are composite to the shaft are not much different from the people who operate at the tip of the spear. We can have some commonalities, can come from similar backgrounds, but it is the choices we make as individuals that make the biggest difference as to where we fall in the spear analogy.

Likewise, there are similar elements between contributors to an organization, but how they are processed (trained) and used (roles) can vary widely in implementation. Knowing what tools you possess, recognizing which position you fill in the grand scheme of things, and understanding the unique value you bring makes all the difference in how you function on a personal and interpersonal level.

Let me address folks who are a component of the shaft but for some reason tend to compare themselves to the tip. While their role is just as important, many struggle to find their value—and potential—in their position as part of the shaft. Instead of striving to learn and grow, seeing challenges as opportunities to develop, they can get caught up in where they aren't or get bogged down in the opinions of those around them.

My advice to you: take full responsibility for the place you're in today while actively pursuing personal development. Your current role can eventually become the pathway to a position at the tip. If you're support, be the best support you can be until you become the supported. In the SEAL Teams alone, I witnessed many sailors who started out as support go off to BUD/S and come back as SEALs themselves.

Effective leadership is often the culmination of years of trial and error and a blending of complementary personalities and skill sets. We are placed in a position based on our potential, so don't be afraid to ask questions, find a mentor, and ask for help when you need it. Be honest and fair—these should be core values. Have the courage to acknowledge your shortfalls and the humility to grow through them. Being refined at any level, including the shaft, prepares us for what's next. No gained knowledge or learned skill set goes to waste in the long run—be open to the process!

A team mentality—a group mindset—is paramount to organizational success. We are often needed where we will make the team the strongest. Your contribution is vital! Even if it is only temporary, it is a time to hone your strengths and to work with and through your weaknesses. Ask yourself, "How can I better myself today in order to be more valuable later?"

As you sharpen your skill set, you'll likely start thinking of ways to improve your organization or implement your increased value within your team. Don't be afraid to voice your ideas to those higher than you along the shaft, or even those at the tip of the spear.

In turn, recognize that even if sometimes management says "no" to your ideas or suggestions, there may be laws or rules that predicate the decisions and mode of operation. Always seek the *why*. Being willing to allow others to lead and guide us through our weaknesses takes humility and courage, but that is what is required to get to your desired destination. While it's not always fun, one simply cannot get better at their craft or in their role unless they are willing to do the work to exceed their current contribution.

You're hired to do a job, and you should strive to be the best that you can be. This doesn't mean you can't aspire to do other things. However, you should be the best at what you're being paid to do while you're there. DO YOUR JOB. People at the tip depend on you being as good at your role as they are at theirs.

Until you migrate to the tip, be the best at what is in front of you.

Likewise, people at the tip need to acknowledge people in support roles who have a "tip of the spear" mindset. Those in the shaft who strive to be the best they can be enhance the overall effectiveness of the folks at the tip. These support folks work just as hard and just as long as the folks at the tip. In many cases, they even work longer and harder. They have different roles but the same mindset.

And realistically, those at the tip can't do it all on their own. They need support personnel to excel. So, it's important that the elite members of any organization acknowledge and appreciate the people in the shaft who are critical to the organization's success—even if in a different way compared to the people at the tip of the spear.

After leaving SEAL Team 6, I took orders for shore duty, which usually means you don't deploy for a while. See, shore duty is like a break from high-tempo operations and usually involves being in some kind of administrative role. This is common in the whole navy, not just the SEAL Teams.

I was in charge of the medical department at Special Boat Unit 20, which supported Naval Special Warfare with boating-type stuff. I was no longer a Team 6 operator but was in an administrative support role for non-SEALs. We had reserve boat guys—full-time civilians and part-time sailors—straight from the fleet (the conventional navy, not Special Warfare). This was before Special Warfare Combat Crewman (SWCC) was the standard for our Naval Special Warfare Boat Teams. A reserve sailor is required to perform two weeks of annual training every year, and this one guy would do his two-week annual training in the medical department because, in his civilian life, he was an EMT.

One day, as I was typing away on administrative stuff, that guy was sitting behind me at a workstation and going on about how he's a SCUBA diver, and he free-fall jumps as a civilian, so he is pretty much the same as I am. A SEAL, in essence.

I picked up a pen from my desk, turned around, and threw it. The pen flew right by his face and stuck into the partition behind him. His eyes widened, and the shock of what I had just done silenced him quickly. I looked him in the eyes and said, "Because we can do that, b*tch!"

Now, I probably couldn't do it again if I tried, and I'm certainly not advocating everyone start throwing ballpoint pens at each other, but the point is I did something. People at the tip of the spear know their place. No questions, no doubt. Unlike this guy, people at the tip have no need to prove their position with words to anyone.

The proof comes from our actions.

LEADERSHIP

Webster's definition of leadership is: "the capacity or ability to lead." Rodney's definition is "the ability to get people to do what they normally wouldn't."

Why is leadership important? Opportunities to lead are all around us. Truth be told, no matter your position within an organization, you lead by example in how you carry yourself, how you engage with others, and whether you do the right thing when nobody's watching. So often, certain positions are coveted because people believe they garner respect (even sometimes without it being truly earned by performance). However, you can lead regardless of your status on paper or position in the org chart. It's your role, not leadership, that gives you responsibilities. Again, mindset makes all the difference in being elite versus simply going through the motions.

Here are some components of leadership, regardless of your job title:

Act courageously, especially when the only thing at stake is people making fun of you.

Fear is an emotional response to a possible negative outcome. In most cases, fear holds people back in the sense that they are more concerned with the potential bad that may outweigh the potential good.

Courage, on the other hand, exists in the presence of fear. It is choosing the right thing because the good is more important than the potential bad.

I once had the opportunity to speak to a group of firefighters. We talked about teamwork, integrity, and leadership. At one point, I was asked how I would address poor behavior at the station house between teammates, seniors, and comrades if the poor behavior had been accepted or tolerated by others. I responded to this young firefighter by saying, "There is no doubt in anyone's mind that firefighters are courageous, but why is it easier to be courageous fighting a fire than correcting a teammate's behavior?"

After a beat, I continued. "The answer is simple: a firefighter is expected to go into harm's way to save lives. Saving a life outweighs the potential dangers of the fire. The risk of being seen as an outcast by your peers doesn't outweigh the benefit of correcting substandard performance or behavior."

Many think it is always management's place to correct bad behavior. The problem is, more often than not, by the time the issue gets to management, it has become a significant problem and potentially a pattern or cultural norm. So, as daunting as it may seem, it's crucial for peers to be transparent with each other and to hold one another accountable. After all, this fear of correcting your peers and ignoring issues can also create cliques within a group—not a great idea if teamwork is vital to your organization's success.

I told the firefighters that the hardest courage to find is when we are faced with what our peers could think of us. This, in my opinion, is when we need to be our most bold. In time, people will usually see that it was the right thing to do. Any ridicule that may follow more than likely comes from them not being courageous enough to put an end to the bullshit in the workplace themselves.

Now, this is not a free ticket to impose your will on others. If you are correcting a discrepancy, you had better be backed by a policy, procedure, directive, or social norm. Personality clashes are not a reason to point out something you don't like. But as long as it's motivated by the right reasons, having the guts to stand up for what's right for the better of the organization is sure to have positive results in the long term, even if it's an intimidating prospect in the short term.

Positional authority and being in charge are two very different and distinct things.

Positional authority usually comes in the form of a doctrine or law that governs a position. If you accept the position, you are now responsible for everything your position governs. Any person can then be assigned a task to be completed at a certain time, to a certain standard, and within the confines of the doctrine or law. If this task is not completed in time, is not completed to standard, or is completed outside the doctrine or law, the person with positional authority is responsible.

Do things get done outside doctrine or law sometimes? Hell yes. This is part of managing risk. Often, those new to positional authority try to control everything. Or worse—they do all the tasks themselves for fear of poor productivity, getting into trouble, or even getting fired. In reality, the fact is that this person with authority probably doesn't have the skill set or know-how to lead effectively. Communication between the one responsible and the one tasked is key. A perfect example of this is in our military services oath of enlistment versus oath of office.

*THE ENLISTED OATH: I (state your name) do solemnly swear
(or affirm) that I will support and defend the Constitution of the
United States against all enemies, foreign and domestic; that I will
bear true faith and allegiance to the same; and that I will obey the orders*

of the president of the United States and the orders of the officers
appointed over me, according to regulations and
the Uniform Code of Military Justice, so help me God.

VS

THE OFFICER OATH: I (state your name) do solemnly swear
(or affirm) that I will support and defend the Constitution of the
United States against all enemies, foreign and domestic; that I will
bear true faith and allegiance to the same; that I take this obligation
freely, without any mental reservation or purpose of evasion; that
I will well and faithfully discharge the duties of the office on which
I am about to enter, so help me God.

Notice the difference? Upon enlisting, a non-commissioned officer (enlisted) swears to obey orders; they are taking an oath of service. The officer, on the other hand, swears to take up the obligation; they are taking an oath to perform the position. This distinction is rarely discussed, but it's the difference between a commissioned officer and a non-commissioned officer.

Now, in no way am I saying that one is more important than the other or that the enlisted are not responsible for their actions. Hell, I did sixteen years as an enlisted man. I am just pointing out that the enlisted are in charge, and the officers are responsible.

The best way to explain this for our non-military readers is to think of a parent teaching a fifteen-year-old son or daughter how to drive a car. The fifteen-year-old is in charge of the car, how fast it goes, where it goes, and when it stops. The parent, however, is responsible for everything that fifteen-year-old does in and with that car. This is not to say the fifteen-year-old is not capable; I'm just pointing out who the courts will go after if something bad happens.

Being a leader has nothing to do with position, rank, title, pedigree, or name. Rather, it's about your personal convictions and integrity. Too often, people misinterpret responsibility or title for good leadership. Would it be great for someone in a position of responsibility to have leadership skills? Yes, but their title does not necessarily make them a true leader.

Furthermore, too often, people look at their bosses and are more than happy to see them fail. But I ask: Where are *your* leadership skills? Where are *your* conviction and integrity? What is *your* responsibility to help your boss succeed? Do you even realize that is your responsibility? If you know that they're heading in the wrong direction or toward failure, why aren't you stepping in as a leader and correcting them or helping guide them to the proper path for the overall success of the organization?

People would often rather see a company fail and then wonder why they're out of a job than step in when they have the opportunity to lead. This is where it's vital to remember that, regardless of your position, your role is a key part of the overall growth, health, and longevity of the organization to which you contribute. Far too often, our misunderstanding of our own value clouds our vision, creating a spirit of internal competitiveness instead of a culture of cooperation.

What matters to you and what you take a vested interest in is ownership.

Now, this to me is an easy concept—one I addressed with my sailors. For some reason, they felt it was easier for me to have ownership because I'm a Navy SEAL and, well, we just don't give up. I told them we all have the same abilities to practice ownership and I could prove it to them.

"How many of you have internet?" I asked. Most of them raised their hands. Then, I added, "How many of you have cable TV?" The rest raised their hands. Next, I asked them, "How long will you stay on the phone to get your internet back up and running?" Hands fell, and I could see some smiles. "How long will you stay on the phone to get your pay-per-view program on the TV after paying for it?" I saw everyone nodding their heads, and a few started to laugh. I pointed out to all of them that *that* is ownership.

It is yours to fix, maintain, make better, whatever. It's yours.

In another group, again speaking about ownership, I did a little exercise. I asked them, "If you are ten miles away from your home and you see an unkempt yard, what do you think? OK, if you turn into your own *neighborhood* and see an unkempt yard, how do you feel? If your *neighbor* next door has an unkempt yard, what are you thinking? If *your* yard looks like shit, what do you think?"

That is ownership.

A leader's job is not to deplete resources but to get the most out of the resources they have. And yes, humans are resources too. In fact, humans are a renewable resource. Don't ever get so full of yourself that you think the team, organization, or company couldn't exist without you. To the decision-makers, don't ever be afraid to divest of useless resources. Just because something has always been doesn't mean it should continue to be today.

Where is the ownership? Stop letting things happen to you. Inject yourself when and if you know better. Let yourself be heard.

I'll illustrate this with an analogy. Picture yourself as a baby eagle resting in a nest, confined to a small area and staying as quiet as you can be to ensure no predators come eat you. You're waiting for mom or dad to show up with whatever they caught for dinner. When one of them arrives with food, you open your mouth as wide as you can to accept whatever they want to jam down your throat. Yes, you are protected, and yes, you are provided for. But you just exist.

Alternatively, you can be that eagle that spreads its wings and gets out of the nest to see the world. You can decide what you are going to eat that evening instead of just waiting to receive whatever shows up. Yes, there is uncertainty. Yes, there is danger. But you're living. You are taking ownership of your future, your well-being, and your life.

The truth is that we are all dying. That is a fact. How many people are truly living? Leaders are not afraid to live. Make a decision to do something. When it is all said and done and I look back on my life, it's the experiences, good or bad, that will make my memories.

Remember, being a leader has nothing to do with position or title. You can be the leader of your one-man army as long as you're out doing something.

Rodney's Trinity of Leadership

To be a good leader, you must be a good follower and a good teacher. To be a good follower, you must be a good teacher and a good leader. To be a good teacher, you must be a good leader and a good follower. Now, I'm talking more about the role than the trait of leadership. In each role of this trinity, you will still find opportunities to be courageous, to be responsible, and to take ownership.

Leading and following go hand in hand. For example, if a leader has no one to follow them, then whom are they leading? Can he or she still be considered a leader? Likewise, if followers have no one to lead them, then whom are they following? Can he or she still be considered a follower?

I will say, however, that some would question how teaching fits into this trinity of leadership. If current leaders don't take the time to invest in and train up tomorrow's leaders, who will? People who have never had the charge of command? Theorists? The problem is . . . theorists are the last ones who should be teaching our future leaders how to lead. Current leaders need to take the time to develop those who will lead tomorrow. If you are asking yourself who the future leaders are, the answer is *everyone* within your organization. Likewise, followers also need to teach the next generation what it means to follow and how to follow well—but not to follow blindly.

If the teaching is done correctly, the teacher learns just as much, if not more, from those being taught. And I know this from personal experience. I never taught a class the same way twice. Why? Because I always learned from the questions my students asked, the things that happened in a controlled environment that I didn't think were possible. Of course, I was also motivated by the desire to make the course better for the next group.

In my own experience, I would say the primary cultural norm that affects my way of teaching is in the category of law enforcement or military personnel. You have to earn their respect. While I'm not saying that you don't have to earn the respect of civilians, I am saying that there is a lot of butt sniffing, for lack of a better term, when you're around people who have similar experiences to mine. I think what breaks down potential barriers is when I tell them that I'm not here to say that the way they do things is wrong; I'm just here to share the way I think.

My perspective is that if how and why I do things is useful, then great! If not, that's fine too.

When you're at the tip, there's an adrenaline rush. It's an experience like no other and is somewhat like an addiction—one that doesn't go away. But, as time moves on, we can't indefinitely maintain that same level of output or action, so we must choose to get back to the basics of being honest and fair about where we are. Having been at the tip, it now becomes my responsibility to turn and shift into a teaching role. I worked my way up; now, I go back to the beginning and help others advance.

*Every generation must choose to make the way for the next
in the natural progression of things.*

Unfortunately, many shy away from this role in the process. Often, it's
a challenge to learn to effectively communicate and overcome the chasm
that can accompany a wide range of personalities, learning styles, generations, and cultural norms. While teaching is not easy, it's actually unnatu-
ral *not* to teach. We are designed to propagate knowledge, to perpetuate
our legacy and cultivate growth.

Many times, however, we look at the next generation's differences
compared to our own generation and are intimidated or turned off. They
use different words, they may not like to hear "should" or "need to," and
they interact largely via text, struggling at times with face-to-face communication. For the younger generation, us oldies seem out of touch and
use antiquated philosophies and systems.

Nonetheless, it's imperative that we take the time to learn to bridge
those gaps, not only to maintain the organization's standards but also to
continue using our finely honed skills (and speak to that still-great need

for action). Our experiences and wealth of knowledge are not meant to be merely kept for ourselves and held just for bragging rights. Rather, we are called to pass along what we have learned to foster growth and continue the cycle. Truly, what is the harm in the next gen being better than us? Isn't that what we inherently desire?

If you treat people as if they can't, they won't. Similarly, if you are allowed to be treated as if you can't, you won't. The responsibility of casting, establishing, and sustaining an organizational goal belongs to everyone.

ASK QUESTIONS

I held command (as a commanding officer) twice. Both times were for shore duty commands—mostly administrative. In this circumstance, we were not the manning priority for the force—and rightly so. In other words, when it came time to staff my group, I wasn't at the top of the list. So, I wasn't getting the most motivated or best sailors in the navy. Also, the navy would fill a ship's vacancy before mine, so if I had a problem with any of my sailors and decided to discipline or get rid of them, I had one less sailor to help with the work of an already under-staffed command. So, how could I take the components of my spear and improve the quality of what I had been given?

I *had* to motivate my sailors—had to shape them and bring the best out in them instead of just bitching about how things sucked. In short, I had what I had. Not a deep bench, and everyone on my staff was juggling multiple programs. (I loved my staff—they were awesome!)

One day, I started noticing a divide among the crew. It was almost right down the middle. This side versus that. My senior enlisted and I watched for a while to see if it would work itself out. It didn't.

I would try to schedule some type of competition each month, and whoever won got a free lunch on me. The competitions were in the form of bake-off or chili cook-off—stuff like that. During the luncheon for the winners, my senior enlisted and I started getting insights into why the staff was divided. What it all came down to was personality differences.

I then remembered that during my commanding officer/executive officer training, each of us had taken a personality test. This test gives you deeper insight into what you like, what you don't like, why you operate as you do, and how your personality responds to and relates with others. I dug through all my paperwork and found my results. What was so great about this was that it helped to reveal the differences in personality in any one command and enabled me to begin to see how we could address some of the team challenges we were experiencing.

We scheduled a meeting with the staff, and I shared my own experience at school, letting them all read my results. I also explained the two biggest personality types were introvert and extrovert. You see, what was being interpreted as dislike or rudeness was really just personalities clashing. Introverts often hate mandatory "fun" like bake-offs or group outings. Extroverts usually love that shit. Extroverts want friends and seek acceptance whereas introverts generally couldn't care less about that.

The takeaway was not to try to change anyone but to inform them of the tendencies of each. We encouraged them not to take anything personally but to recognize that they had aligned themselves based on personality. There really was no need for an "us versus them" culture. Rather, I presented it as an opportunity to recognize and honor the differences in personalities. Asking someone to join you for lunch (extroverts) and getting told "no" (by introverts) was not a big deal. No one was angry or hating on the extroverts; many introverts would just rather eat lunch alone. Conversely, to introverts, an extrovert extending an invitation was not them trying to get under anyone's skin; extroverts just want to include everyone.

The better an organization understands personality types, the better prepared it is to handle innocent encounters between team members. Be willing to be curious, to ask questions. Use tools like personality tests and be open to learning new forms of communication. The varying personality types and tendencies bring great strength to your organization if you are willing to identify them, value them, and learn to work together for that common goal.

Like a spear, many different components are arranged together to create a whole. Each component has a different beginning, a different way of preparing for best use, and a different role. Nonetheless, every part has to be respected and treated according to what works for it. For instance, you wouldn't use a sharpening stone on your shaft. Likewise, you wouldn't use wood stain on your spearhead.

Know your people.

COMMAND AND CONTROL

When considering what determines the command and control of the spear as the weapon, we can consider the hand that guides it. If the hand is positioned too close to the spearhead, you lose the full ability of the spear—you gain more accuracy but give up reach. Alternately, when you place your hand at the very end of the spear, you may not be as accurate, but you can cover more distance. As the wielder becomes more confident, they will find that sweet spot on the spear shaft to make them the most effective.

The manner in which our military engages around the world may surprise many of you. We have the commander in chief of the military (the president), the Joint Chiefs of Staff (senior-most military members who act as advisors), and combatant commanders (four-star admirals or generals responsible for military operations in their section of the world). All the commands back in the US are force providers to the combatant commanders. This understanding helped cement the spear analogy in my mind because it was clear then whose hand was guiding the spears provided to any given region of the world for the military.

I share this with you to challenge you to be aware of the hand that guides your spear, regardless of the organization you find yourself in. It may surprise you. A dad, an artist, and a writer working at the tip of the spear are all ultimately guided by someone else: a dad by his family, an artist by their fans, a writer by their readers.

More importantly, this understanding may also clarify some of the more vague or puzzling procedural implementations that we can sometimes struggle with when a clear overarching objective is absent. When we operate with unanswered questions like, "Why the hell are we doing it this way?" or, "This doesn't make sense," we can battle with internal frustrations that often filter to those around us, bringing dissension or worse—division. Find the end user, and you'll more often than not find your answers.

The hand, too, is guided. It is connected to an arm and so on until you get to the brain where decisions are made. There is input from the hand, arm, and shoulder as to the likes and dislikes of the spear, but the decision is still made in the brain. What does the spear (end product) look and feel like? Is the shaft too big for my hand? Is the spearhead too heavy for the strength in my forearm? Do I like the color?

As with everything, spears must be created to the specifications of what the welder desires, likes, or requires. Who wants to bust his or her ass becoming something no one wants or even needs?

I have been asked: what determines the health of an organization? This is tricky. Some would focus on morale or earnings. Some would say that the health of an organization is determined by how well the overall goals and strategies are communicated and implemented, including a culture of ownership.

I say the health of an organization is evidenced by how long the organization survives. Survival is not a bad word. We survive every day. Which metrics dictate how long an organization is around involve everything. Sometimes, you have to cut things back to keep the whole healthy, while at other times, you need to add. Once the end goal is established and teams operate in unity, day-to-day implementation becomes clearer. Those in command, like it or not, control the longevity of an organization.

You must stay relevant in your space, job, or discipline—or be left behind to become a relic or one of many "remember when" stories that inevitably become distant memories.

THE STRENGTH OF THE SPEAR
(OR SHAFT)

Similar to the process the steel goes through when it is forged through heat and pressure, the shaft goes through its own crucible in the quest to find the right balance in being effective.

Is it too brittle? A brittle shaft is one that is too hard with very little flexibility. It will break easily when stressed. It may be very straight and accurate for the end user, but how many times can you use that hard, brittle shaft before it breaks, leaving the spearhead operationally ineffective?

At the other end of the spectrum is a very flexible shaft. This shaft may be so flexible that it bends under the weight of the spearhead. While it is more resilient and will probably bend on impact, it's not as effective because it's not delivering the spear tip to its intended target, which will either force the wielder to grasp the shaft closer to the spearhead (sacrificing reach) or cause the wielder to perform extra thrusts (additional work/energy) in order to hit the target.

While this loss of reach and extra work may not be a big deal to this particular shaft, giving up reach negates half of the shaft's abilities. Plus, creating more work for the spearhead reduces the life span of the spear tip. A sharp tip or cutting edge is always slightly deformed after each impact or use, requiring more sharpening and honing. Sharpening never adds steel; it always *removes* steel. The shaft should never lose sight of that fact.

From an organizational perspective, this analogy can manifest in management in two ways: micromanaging or disengaged leadership.

A micromanaging culture is one in which leadership is constantly judging its workers in every aspect of the workday, or the consequences are great if you make an honest mistake. "Why were you two minutes late today?" "You take too many breaks." "You can submit better products than this." "You haven't met your quota for the week." "Why aren't you at your desk?" The list goes on. This can create a very rigid workplace (having a very hard shaft, being too stiff or brittle), which will cause your organization to break easily when stressed. It may survive one or even two very stressful events, but eventually, it will break.

Think about it this way: Glass is harder than steel. Glass is so hard it is brittle and breaks easily when stressed.

A disengaged manager practicing too flexible of leadership sounds more like this: "Do what you want." "Don't ask me." "I'll be late tomorrow." "I'm working from home this week." "That's OK that this product sucks; you'll get it next time." This type of manager gets taken advantage of and very seldom has employees complain—until targets are missed. That's when the finger pointing starts. A very soft shaft is too flexible or not as accurate and will cause your organization to not care when stressed. Eventually, the organization will fail when clients realize the hard work and discipline are lacking, and they'll go elsewhere to find something better.

To put this into perspective, lead can be shaped into a spearhead, but lead is too soft to hold an edge, so the spear tip will bend under pressure. Lead is also very toxic and kills slowly. Missing intended targets will slowly kill an organization like lead.

Proper balance is key.

NEW GUY

During my first deployment back in 1988, my platoon mate and I launched early in order to turn over (pass on info, equipment, etc.) with the platoon in-country. While doing so, we joined the second platoon on a trip. It was a training mission with the local forces. The air force base was located in the center of the country, and our training site was on the coast.

All of us, plus all our gear, were flying out to the site when the Chinook had to perform an emergency landing as warning alarms started going off. Thankfully, the pilot found a clearing and landed safely. They were able to dispatch Hueys to ferry personnel to the training site, but the

Chinook with all the gear had to stay the night until mechanics could get out there and fix the bird. My platoon mate and I stood watch, as we were straphangers (extra bodies) anyway. The night was interesting but, for the most part, uneventful.

The next day, we reconnected with second platoon and continued with the training mission. Two weeks later, another Chinook was five minutes out from picking us up and moving us back to the air force base when it crashed and killed everyone on board. The Chinook fleet was grounded. Now, we had to figure out how to get all our gear back to the base before our C5 (cargo plane) headed back to home base. The OIC was already thinking about rolling back to the States and came up with a *brilliant* plan.

"Rodney, you look local. Go out in town and hire a truck big enough for all our gear, and you can drive our stuff back to the base. We leave in three days. Try to make it. If you don't, we'll see you when you get back."

OK, so I'm the twenty-year-old new kid, my Spanish sucks, and there is a war going on. I got this.

With my pistol in tow, civilian clothes on, and a fist full of cash, I hired a truck and driver. We loaded it up, covered it as best we could, and set off.

The truck was old, the tires were bald, and if there was gravel on the road, we considered it an improvement. Twenty miles an hour was pushing the limits of this vehicle. Every time the driver sped up, the tires would heat up, a rock would puncture one of them, and we'd have a flat to fix. This was normal for the truck crew because they had plenty of spares— just as bald as the ones they replaced but at least holding air.

After thirty-six hours of slow going in the middle of nowhere, I started accepting the fact that I may be stuck in that country for a while. Then, it came to me. In my broken Spanish, I convinced the driver to speed up. I knew the risk with the tires, but I told him, "Remember the guy who was giving us orders?" He said yes. I told the driver, "He has your money, and he is leaving tomorrow."

Actually, I had the money, and yes, I had already thought about commandeering the truck at gunpoint by then. I didn't know the landscape, however, and maps were useless anyway because most of the roads had been destroyed due to the war. I needed the driver more than he needed me. But I had to influence his thinking. Money did the trick.

We rolled in late morning, and I was sure the platoon had already left. To my surprise, I saw my platoon mate as we entered the base. He told me we had to hurry and get the gear on pallets, then get them inspected and loaded on the plane.

"I thought for sure that you had already left!" I commented in disbelief.

"We were going to, but the remains of the crew from the Chinook that went down are traveling back with us, and they're holding a ceremony for them."

With that, we got busy. I paid the driver, and we headed back to our home for the next seven months. Welcome to the Teams, New Guy!

Here's the truth of it and the crux of the story. One could look at that situation and think, "Man, he was just a kid! What a jerk his OIC was to send him out to fail!" Truth is, back then, I wasn't sure I was ready to take on that huge of a task. The way I see it now, though, is that my OIC trusted that even if *I* didn't think I had what it took, *he* saw someone who could rise to the occasion. If things hadn't worked out as planned, he believed I would come out on the other side stronger and more aware of my own capabilities.

Back in the day, teens and young adults were running households and sprinting into battle, while so many kids today are seen as incapable. Many miss the truth that even as young humans, we are capable of way more than we are often given the opportunity to discover. Unfortunately, in an effort to let our children "have a childhood," I believe in a lot of ways we've set them up to fail. To many, adulting seems overwhelming, and responsibility seems foreign.

People will live up to the expectations we set before them. If, at first, they stumble, then use this as a teaching opportunity. Never, ever leave them with the impression that they can't or that they're incapable. If you do, you will soon find yourself overworked and alone. It may take more of your time to teach them and more effort on their part to get where they need to be, but eventually, they will get it done. It may not be to your standards at first, but like making a spear, it will take several times before you get it just right.

ANY JOB CAN LEAD TO OPPORTUNITIES

Achieving a goal is like running a marathon. We are each born with different skill sets and grow up with various resources and opportunities. Consequently, while some may only have ten miles ahead of them, many run the twenty-six miles and 385 yards, and still others may have to run forty miles. In the end, however, the finish line remains the same. Regardless of what that is for each of us or how much training or equipment we have had access to, in all scenarios, it takes effort to finish the race. Talent, economic class, friends, and social networks all affect the so-called distance in this analogy, but the goal line remains constant.

And truly, we all have a shot at finishing the race.

I was a little bit of what you would call a helicopter parent when I was home. I didn't want our kids to want for anything or feel embarrassed like I did growing up. When I was a child, my own clothes were hand-me-downs from four older brothers, and I had to work hard at the jobs I had to provide for my family. As an adult, I chose an industry, a career, where as long as I kept performing, I had job security. Consistency in provision meant everything to me, and that translated into my parenting as well.

While it's been important to me to provide resources and prevent our kids from experiencing lack, I believe we also successfully strove to show them that hard work and intentionality are key. They don't have to start way at the back of the line like others do because they know they are safe and provided for, but they do need to recognize that they still have to give it their all to achieve what they want to in this life.

We all gotta run that race.

When I decided to leave active duty, I was accepted by the US Marshal Service. I had to wait for an academy date before I was hired, and of course, you have to graduate from the academy before you receive your commission. Unfortunately, as my enlistment was ending, the Marshal Service went into a hiring freeze. I asked the command master chief if I could extend my enlistment six months due to the hiring freeze, and his answer was no. However, I could reenlist for three years.

I don't blame him—he didn't want me to get out, as he had the health of the force to think about. But now what? Stay in and go back to one of my old SEAL Teams? Get back on the deployment cycle for another six years?

Could my family even survive this?

The recruiter from the Marshal Service seemed to believe the freeze wouldn't last that long and we would be back to normal by the next quarter, so I decided to get out. I had to take into consideration the potential strain on my family. Whether my wife stayed with me would not be based on the Teams but rather based on my effort—or lack thereof. At least, that's what I thought at the time. (Don't be sad—we are still together and going strong.)

This short-lived freeze ended up lasting longer than I could wait. I had a family to provide for, so I started applying to other federal law enforcement agencies. We were living in south Texas because we had family support there, and at the time, my wife was licensed in Texas as a dental hygienist. The Drug Enforcement Administration (DEA) showed interest in me and invited me to an interview at their Dallas office. So, now I needed to buy a suit for this interview—a.k.a first impression. Where to go? Men's Wearhouse, obviously. ("You'll like the way you look.") So, off I went with family in tow to buy a suit.

As we were shopping, I realized the prices were fair but a little more than I could afford at the time. I asked the salesperson if there was an employee discount. She replied, "Oh, yes. A really good one." So, I inquired whether they were hiring. She asked me if I was serious, and I said, "Hell, yes!" I needed to work, and when the marshals did call, I would need nice clothes for the job.

She handed me an application, and that very day, I interviewed with the manager. He offered me the position on the spot and asked when I could start. I told him I had a long bus ride the next day for my interview, but I could start when I got back. Bus ride, change in bathroom, interview, poly test, change in bathroom, bus ride back to the Rio Grande Valley, start work.

I was not a salesman but rather a helper/entry-level employee. I learned how to match outfits, accessorize, and fold clothes. I was completely happy working for eight dollars an hour and getting a deep discount on clothes.

One day, George Zimmer (the founder) visited our store. Mr. Zimmer made it a point to visit all his locations at least once a year. I was busy keeping the store picked up and putting things in their place when he approached me and asked what I was doing. Of course, I immediately thought I was doing something wrong. Noting the expression on my face, he qualified his question and asked, "*Why* are you working here?"

I told him that I liked the clothes, and the employee discount was great. He laughed and then shared that the manager had told him I was a Navy SEAL. He was curious as to why now I had such an interest in menswear. The light bulb turned on, and I understood the line of questioning.

I told him I was in transition from the military, and my wife and I had a newborn. My wife worked two days a week, and I worked five, so one of us was always home with our daughter. Mr. Zimmer then asked me if I wanted to manage my own store. He shared that he was impressed I would be just as enthusiastic working at the entry level in one of his stores as I was being a SEAL.

I graciously declined his offer, explaining that as soon as the Marshal Service or DEA offered me a job, I was going to take it. "It wouldn't be fair to you, sir, if I accepted the position to leave shortly after." He understood, and we parted with Mr. Zimmer saying, "If you change your mind, give me a call."

Work is out there. How you *think* about work, however, is what leads to opportunities. Mr. Zimmer was looking at his spear. He saw me in the shaft working to the best of my abilities, and he thought I would be better suited somewhere in the spearhead and could maybe one day even work my way to the tip. He was willing to take a chance on me, not because I knew the ins and outs of menswear but because I was willing to do what it took to be successful in that position. I wasn't "too good" to fold clothes; the work and pay were not beneath me. At that time, the measure of my success was being able to provide for my family. That was all.

I feel that if most people made this one small shift in how they view work, it would catapult production, achievement, and even quality to greater heights for not only the organization in which they operate but also themselves. That small change is this: don't categorize it.

Work is work.

"Easy work," "hard work," or "dirty work"—honestly, it's all the same. If it has to be done, then do it. Don't bitch that it's shitty work. It's just work. Don't elevate or diminish a position (or person) based on your personal evaluation of the job at hand. Furthermore, teamwork is just *team* and *work*. No adverbs or hyphens in front. Just work.

If you choose to make that small change in perspective, you'll do it all, do it well, and be a person companies want to keep. In fact, you'll be a person people want to be around. Don't underestimate the value of that.

WHEN FREE GETS TOO EXPENSIVE

When people forget what has been done for them, begin expecting favors as normal, or start being asses to those who help them out, I refer to that mindset as "when free gets too expensive"—for both parties. When working on a team, it's essential that everyone pitches in and uses their strengths to support each other in reaching a common goal. One-sided work relationships contribute to poor morale and even worse productivity.

When those who are lending their strength or resources are treated poorly, it creates a deficit in that person's worth and causes a potential breakdown in effectiveness. And those on the receiving end who refuse to reciprocate not only miss out on the opportunity to contribute common courtesy but to actually challenge the team dynamic. Subsequently, they are robbed of the personal development required to further their own goals as well as corporate potential.

This is a mindset issue on both sides—for both the person doing the favor and the person receiving the help.

Now, a word for the decision-makers: evaluate your day-to-day outside of work. Take note of the pleasant versus the negative experiences of the places you frequent or your personal choice of entertainment (i.e., sports, movies, etc.) You will notice that organizations that are staffed effectively are pleasant. Meanwhile, those that are staffed poorly, well, suck.

Too many hiring decisions are based on favors or having the right mix of race, gender, whatever. When hiring or promoting employees, a decision-maker's focus should be on what is best for the organization. People who work in roles that don't speak to their capabilities or contribute to the organization's efficiency are likely to lean into the lying, hiding, and faking that create weakness in the spear.

Intentionality in the hiring and pairing of team members and team leads can change the entire dynamic of the group. It also has a great impact on how effective the team is in pursuing organizational goals. If you hired the employee for X, let them focus on X. With morale high, you will find your employees helping each other gladly with little drama, creating a positive atmosphere for everyone involved. The difference is in someone being expected to help versus being willing to help without being asked. Their mindset and attitude change completely. Remember, a favor is no longer a favor when it is expected.

Whether you are creating a united atmosphere for incoming clientele or formulating a team of kick-ass warriors headed into battle, who and how individuals are trained and teamed up can determine whether there is a cohesive mentality. These may also be the determining factors contributing to the organization's success or utter failure—or even great loss. Like-minded individuals fully aware of their own and their team members' strengths and weaknesses, partnered with a clear understanding of their particular role, can make all the difference.

I was in the Middle East working for the CIA. Leaving the Marshal Service and joining the agency gave me the same sensation as when I left SEAL Team 4 and checked into an even more elite SEAL Team. It was like leaving the minor league and being brought up to the show—the majors. I say this not because the people are any more or less capable but because of the operating tempo, support, equipment, and budgetary differences between the two. In one organization, we were counting pennies; the other organization was making it rain. I am not implying that money was wasted, but there was just a lot less red tape. If you could articulate a need for gear or training, it was more effectively supported at the show, and we got busy.

Anyway, I was in the Middle East, and I realized how many locals we had working for us on any given day—completing mundane tasks like cooking, cleaning, and mechanical stuff. We also had interpreters. I treated them fairly and asked a few of them if they would help me learn

Farsi. One, so I could blend in out and about. Two, because I noticed that during mealtimes, the locals had their own table, were usually fed after the Americans ate, and more importantly, had better food. (The Americans were getting sick and dropping like flies—literally risking their health because they were "too good" to eat with the locals.) We were eating from the local economy, and even today, I could not identify the meat we were being served. (Honestly, I think it was the ass knuckle of the local goats. They didn't have tails but rather butt flaps, so it had to be the ass knuckle. Sorry—so many memories . . .)

So anyway, one day, I saw one of the Americans going off on one of the local guys. It was about something stupid like not having a car ready—nothing mission critical or even mission enhancing for that matter. I pulled him aside and told him to calm down. "Remember that we are foreigners here; we exist and are safe as long as our hosts allow it," I said. (Before any engagement, the agency was really good at giving us a must-read list. One thing I remember from the required reading was the history of where we were. Once we had worn out our welcome, the use of poison was not out of the question.)

This American's reply to me was, "I'm not a foreigner—I'm an American."

I looked intently at him and said, "We are in the Middle East."

He simply repeated himself. "I'm not a foreigner—I'm an American."

I said, "Well, that is great in America, but we are not there. We are outnumbered and at their mercy."

He turned and walked away, repeating himself once again.

This guy was stuck, and he clearly didn't get it.

Wherever you find yourself, be aware that we are all connected. Take note of who you connect with, recognize who you don't connect with and why, and be aware of the space you are in. It is so important to understand where everyone you are working with is coming from. Understanding and respecting the roles each person plays in the whole changes the mindset of the individual and cultivates the prevailing culture.

MINDSET

Being hard, strong, and tough are not the same.

Hard: not easily penetrated, not easily yielding to pressure

Strong: having or marked by great power

Tough: capable of enduring strain, hardship, or severe labor

All are good to have, but of the three, toughness is what matters most if you're going to reside at the tip of the spear. If you are happy being anywhere but the tip, be strong enough to own that position and do the hard work to stay there.

Some would look at my upbringing and throw out the trauma flag. For me, use of the ideology of trauma is an act of personal destruction. To be honest, it was my childhood hardships that helped build the man I am today, so it is hard for me to see where the trauma was. I guess the takeaway is you can allow negative experiences to destroy part of you, or you can use those same experiences to build something stronger.

I was talking with a young adult the other day, and she was reflecting on a family visit she had just returned from. She made a comment about how someone had made some comment, and now she wanted nothing to do with that person. The offending comment had not been a direct attack toward her—more of a weak attempt at a joke that had bombed.

I mentioned that her generation uses words like "die" and "kill yourself" jokingly, but to me, in this current environment, I take those words and phrases very seriously. I shared that I grew up with adults telling me, "Sticks and stones may break your bones, but words can never hurt you," and pointed out that it's almost as if this current generation prefers sticks and stones rather than words.

She very keenly replied, "But words can be powerful."

"Yes, words can be powerful, but where is that power coming from? The power comes from you. If you allow the words to move you or dictate your actions, *you* are giving those words power. The power given is either in the form of negative emotions or in the form of positive and inspirational emotions."

At the end of the day, I believe we ourselves are the regulators of what power we give and what power we receive.

This power regulation also applies to people. If you allow someone to control your negative responses and emotions, you are giving them power and draining yours. If that person motivates or elicits positive emotions, they are charging you. The point is that YOU decide—not them.

Being the tip of the spear or elite in the way you think transcends the whole of the spear.

My main takeaway is to consider adjusting the way you think. If I can change how someone looks at challenges, then I have made a difference. Changing someone's perspective lasts longer than showing him or her how to do something. Eventually, anyone I've had the pleasure of teaching or mentoring may not have the need to perform what I taught or shared with them, but if I changed their thinking, no matter what they face in the future, they will hopefully be better prepared to handle it.

I will add that because I instruct the same way across the board, I have found that sometimes I turn off people who are not in my profession. For example, I have neighbors who knew nothing or little about firearms and asked if I would teach them. I agreed and worked with them for a few nights. I was starting from the ground floor and explained to them that a fight is a fight—all weapons do is extend your range. I suggested that they take up some kind of striking or grappling art and get used to being hit because of the circumstances that would actually cause them to deploy their weapon.

From my short time in law enforcement, I told them that just because you have the right to carry does not mean you have the right to use. This led me to ask, "What is that line in the sand that someone has to cross to get you to pull your weapon? Where is that line that moves you to pull the trigger?" Training with my neighbors ended shortly after. I was too intense for their simple objective to just carry.

I was asking basic questions that most people who want to carry don't think about. Here is the truth though—just because someone is yelling at me does not give me the right to shoot them. Am I really prepared to go there if need be? I sure am, but I also understand that my life or someone else's life has to be at risk before I use deadly force.

In reality, most people like the idea of carrying a weapon (or holding a position of authority), but they don't want to make the effort of being responsible with that weapon (taking on possible repercussions). We must ask ourselves whether we merely like the idea of carrying a weapon (holding the power, making the decisions) or are willing to fully engage with it.

Similarly, we often want the position, or power, but without taking on that responsibility, training, and renewed mindset ourselves. Being the point of maximum pressure sounds awesome until you start to be sharpened and honed.

This leads me to a saying that I despise: "*Fake it till you make it.*" I had never heard this until I was in the officer ranks, and it did not sit well with me at all. Now, I hear it said far too often by influencers, role models, and celebrities. What a horrible message to send to anyone.

"Why?" you might ask. I'll explain. If I fake it to make it to my desired position, now what? Now I must continue living a lie. Or is the definition of "making it" being in a position to do nothing because that is what would probably be best for the organization? Let's not even get into the disservice to all those who worked hard and did not "fake it" who now have to pick up your slack.

People are promoted based on future potential. Don't fake it till you make it. You'll find that the same amount of effort will be eventually expended in continuing your lies rather than if you had just learned your role in the first place. Instead, challenge yourself to put the effort in. Work your ass off till you make it. That's how you get to the tip of the spear.

REDEFINING SUCCESS

What is success? This is an interesting question. To many people, success is defined by accomplishing a mission or meeting company goals, but for me, it is when the people you have had the privilege and honor to lead would want you to lead them again.

Ultimately, success starts internally. It begins with the right mindset.

Unfortunately, however, many times, success is achieved at the cost of the people you were responsible for or who you were leading. Sure, you may have accomplished that objective or finished a project, but what about down the road? Are you going to have the same people with you for the next one? Do the people who got you moving forward still want to go with you? The difference in mindset comes by evaluating what is more important to you: your people or your project? This is a question we should ask often when we need to make a difficult decision.

An example could be the war in Afghanistan. Once bin Laden was on the run and the Taliban was pushed out of all the major cities, the goal was to create a new democratic authority that would prevent the Taliban from returning to power. Many Americans and our allies rushed to join the fight. Twenty years later, the Taliban regained power in Afghanistan. Today, military recruitment and retention is low, and I heard on the news that Congress is considering reinstating the selective service—in other words, the draft.

Now, the military is inherently dangerous, but as a military leader, you still do whatever possible to tip the scale in your favor to avoid or reduce any losses. From a civilian point of view, are you willing to sacrifice self-centered motives for corporate team goals? It always comes down to the big picture and who is willing to keep that at the forefront of their decision-making.

What condition is your spear in? Can it be used in the next battle? If you have multiple spears and you don't mind breaking a few, how long can you fight until you are left with no spear at all?

Again, in my opinion, success in one battle, challenge, or task involves taking people with you to the next one.

We were doing a night move to meet an asset in town. Two-car package, no armor on the vehicles. We felt speed and agility were more important at night. The streets were pretty empty.

Coming to a long straightaway, I saw a dump truck on the right side of the road. It looked like it was running—the lights on the truck were on, and I could see exhaust coming out the back. I was driving the lead vehicle and got on the radio to call out the potential threat and to say that I was going to speed up and break left. Sure as shit, that dump truck tried to pull out in front of us to block the road. Because we had anticipated this as a potential ambush, I had already started moving all the way over to the left, now in the oncoming traffic lane, which forced the dump truck to pull forward even more and hit the back end of my vehicle as he tried to stop me.

I got around the truck, but even better, the following vehicle broke right and had a clear path of travel behind the dump truck. The mission to meet the asset was aborted, and a successful night was now determined by making our way back to base with no injuries and no loss of personnel. Was this the only ambush waiting for us? Did the person we were going to meet set us up? There were too many unknowns to continue as if nothing had happened.

After making our way back to base and dropping off the person we were protecting, we recruited more guns and went back out looking for these guys. There were dents and broken windows, but our vehicle was still operational. There wasn't a lot of chatter on the radio; everyone did what needed to be done. We weren't shaken up; in fact, we laughed about how obvious this dump truck was in the middle of the night, not picking up trash with the engine running.

Although the mission for that night had been canceled, ultimately turning into hunting for that dump truck, it was still a success that none of us got hurt (except maybe our feelings and the back end of my SUV). At that particular moment, I had made my decision: my people were more important than my project.

TAKE A TACTICAL PAUSE

A *tactical pause* is a moment or two taken to step back when we find ourselves in the heat of things. This allows us to gather our thoughts, effectively assess the situation, and make a good decision (or at least an educated one).

Webster's Dictionary defines an emotion as "a conscious mental reaction (such as anger or fear) subjectively experienced as a strong feeling, usually directed toward a specific object and typically accompanied by physiological and behavioral changes in the body." For the purpose of this conversation, I prefer Webster's simpler definition: "a state of feeling."

I believe that while we are awake, we are constantly in a state of feeling—happy, sad, anxious, fearful, cautious, bored, etc. I also believe feelings are a bit like a two-year-old—kicking, screaming, and crying to reach their goal, not thinking of the consequences, affordability, common courtesy, or even potential health concerns involved in reaching it.

I think we would all agree that we wouldn't let a toddler make life-altering decisions, so then why do so many of us allow our feelings to get the best of us, causing us to do things we normally would not? Road rage, junk food, a new ride . . . I'm guilty of it all. I'm angry, I'm hungry, and damn, that car looks good. When facing overwhelming emotions, however, it's wise to take that tactical pause; think of the second-, third-, or fourth-order effect of the possible action or reaction—and *then* move forward.

I get it—emotions are powerful, and like powerful words, where does the power come from? It comes from you. *You* decide which emotions receive more power. Moreover, you decide when and if to act upon said emotion. In order to attain an elite mindset—one that will have you performing at the tip of the spear at work and in life—you have to learn to set your emotions aside.

We are always in a state of feeling—what matters is what we do in that state.

In the workplace, losing control of your power and allowing others to feed on your emotions can lead to you making poor decisions. It can even result in you losing your job or, worse yet, an injury or even death. And there are potential life-or-death ramifications in other scenarios, such as when serving our country overseas, as well.

On one of my deployments to the Middle East, we were stationed in a place where the food was much better and the living conditions were slightly improved. We had a small contingent of agency folks. From the GRS side of the house, it was one other guy and me. We were just doing our thing, but one day, we found ourselves in the middle of an ambush. Nothing serious, though, and we were able to drive out of it, cars shot up with no one hit and only a few hurt feelings.

When we got back to base, we put things away and wrote our reports. I grabbed my rifle and told my guy I was headed up to the roof to look for targets of opportunity, like people placing IEDs or hasty mortar/rocket attacks. It was during Ramadan, so everyone was restless.

While up on the roof, we spotted a man and his two sons in a boat fishing with nets on the river. Still under the influence of the emotion of the afternoon, my associate wanted to shoot them. I told him, "NO. They are not armed or even looking our way. Besides, the Marines have a checkpoint set up on the river just down the way."

He still wanted to shoot, spouting rules of engagement and saying, "If they are on the river, we can shoot them." I told him no again and forced him off the roof. The father and son kept fishing, were checked by the Marines, and went about their business.

Now, some of you may think I messed up, and maybe I did by going up on the roof in the first place after being ambushed and having my panties all in a wad. But in that moment, I made a choice—one I still stand by today. We are liberators, not murderers. Unlike the anger stirring in my comrade, I was not going to turn a family of unknowns into new enemies of the US because I wanted payback. Period.

Take that tactical pause.

NORMAL GUY

S o many people don't believe they can do great things. They look at their "normal" lives and yearn for something to believe in, something to fight for. Action movies, stories of war and battle, simultaneously stir something deep within us while also putting a mirror up to the often mundane life we experience day in and day out.

But what if we were to redefine doing something "great"? To re-evaluate success and the value of our lives in the undefined time we have?

When I first began to consider writing a book, it was largely because so many people were fascinated by what I had to say. Although many were in awe of what I had accomplished (and some even thought I was making things up), what I found so interesting was how normal I saw my "accomplishments" as being. I could also see the value in sharing the life lessons I have learned through trial, error, and tenacity.

I've realized that while so many, including myself, want to be at the tip of the spear, many more don't recognize their own value and potential. As I've described, as a culture, we tend to miss the fact that the tip is absolutely useless without the shaft. The truth is that the spear without the hand to guide it is useless. Even where and how a spear is held greatly determines its reach and effectiveness.

At every connection point (position, occupation), there is value, and without one another, greatness cannot be achieved.

When I would come home from being deployed, I'd find great peace in building things around the house. In our line of work, the fighting, or getting ready for a fight, never stops—there is never truly an end. When I got home, putting up a fence or working on the basement brought consistency and created an environment of small victories. An end, per se. If the task was done well, it would need no more or very little attention from me again.

As I adjusted to daily life, the values that had gotten me through years in the workplace more clearly affected my approach to my family and home life.

Civilian life is different—extremely different—from military life. I had to adjust my idea of what success looks like and had to discover where I fit into the scheme of things. Similarly, whether we are looking at familial dynamics, career objectives, leadership value, or military engagement, all require authentic assessment and an objective evaluation of the value we bring to any given role. Does the tip of the spear change? Absolutely. Nothing that is living and active remains stagnant; it's imperative to understand and take ownership of our particular place in any given moment or within any organization.

At the end of the day, being at the tip is a mindset, a value. As a young man, I thought the tip of the spear was a place, and in some aspect, it is. But when I reached that place, I quickly realized that the real work had just begun. No time to cheer my accomplishment. No pats on the back. Time to prove to the others who resided at the tip with me that I belonged. Being welded and sharpened, welded and sharpened, I started to realize that how I thought of where I was, was more important than the actual space I occupied. What was expected of me? The rest of the spear was counting on me to do and be the best.

When the time came to migrate down to the shaft, my mind was already set. *I can still be the tip of what I am asked to do or where I am asked to reside. I am no longer battling behind enemy lines but instead fighting against Mother Nature in my yard and for health in my relationships.* It's only natural to make situations and circumstances about ourselves, but we find our self-worth, our value and motivation, when we look outward.

I may not be able to change the world, but perhaps I can make a life-changing difference for one person. Choosing humility, seeking information, and asking questions allow us to fully engage in perpetual growth. It takes intentionality, but that is what feeds our souls and keeps us going. Today, Rodney the husband, father, and friend is just as sharp and active as Rodney the SEAL—same passion, same intensity, different field.

Still at the tip.

CONCLUSION

When I was at commanding officers' school, one of the exercises we were assigned was to develop command philosophies, which a lot of us, including myself, were struggling to do. One student after another would get up to share their philosophies, all of which were along the lines of honor, courage, and commitment. I thought to myself, *These are more values than they are philosophies.* This made me think hard about what a philosophy really is.

To me, it is a set of values and beliefs that guide my choices, responses, and attitude. They are a compilation of how I was raised, what I have experienced, and what I believe to be true. I think it's invaluable to identify and define your personal philosophy, as it can guide you in the day-to-day. Not only that, but when you know what you truly value, it helps you to make decisions based on whether they are aligned with your truest self.

In short, philosophy is a basic belief. With that understanding, I asked myself, *What do I believe in? What guides me in my decision-making? What motivates me to do what I do?*

I think it's worth pointing out how valuable and important everyone is to someone in some shape or form. It's crucial to stop focusing on what you're not or who you aren't and take some time to realize what you ARE and why you MATTER. It could be as simple as being someone's best friend. Someone who listens. Someone who's always there to provide that well-timed hug or that annoying, "I told you so."

We influence more people around us than we will ever know. **Be honest and fair.** Not just to the people around you but also to yourself.

So often we hold ourselves back, placing ourselves in a certain economic class or social group and coming to the conclusion that, "I can't do that. People who do *that* are special." People like to think that the folks at the tip of the spear, in special groups, or at the pinnacle of any discipline are cut from a different cloth. The reality is, however, that we're normal people putting in the hard work, making the sacrifices, and working together to accomplish extraordinary things.

If it has been done before, then why not you? If something is doable, do it. I never thought my background was what the SEALs were looking for until I became one. I never perceived I was officer material until I became an officer. Federal law enforcement? "Surely this is a long shot"... until it wasn't. CIA—the best and the brightest? *This can't possibly be me.* Until it was. Commanding officer—who, me?! Yep. Husband? Still going strong. Awesome dad? Well, that is yet to be determined. My personal measure of success concerning that is: when my kids have kids, do they want me around? That's when I'll know whether I was a good dad. Other dads have different measurements, and that's OK too.

Be who you say you are. If you are a teacher, be a teacher. Understand what being a teacher means. Regardless of your job title, it is just as important that you are the best in that position as any other job in the organization. If you want to do something else, change your job or earn a promotion, but until then, be the best you can be where you are.

Another tip: find people who have gone to places you want to go or achieved whatever it is you're interested in and ask for their advice. Don't look to someone who's never been a doctor and ask him or her what it takes to be a doctor. Find experts in your desired position and ask them how they got to where they are. You'll find that most people will be more than willing to share their stories with you. Those stories are your roadmaps.

I would say that because I came from humble beginnings and have come to realize that my social class or economic status had very little to do with my personal outcome, I am just as comfortable cleaning toilets as I am writing policies or sitting in a boardroom.

Nothing is beneath me, and nothing is out of reach.

Be where your feet are—fully present and committed to the task, meeting, training session, or conversation at hand. Your job and the people around you deserve your undivided attention, just as you deserve theirs.

In a nutshell, those are my main personal philosophies. I encourage all of you to identify your own. Really find what makes you tick. If you are happy with what you discover, drive on. If, for some reason, you are a little disappointed, fix that shit. Nothing is set in stone. Self-reflection is the first step to true growth.

The tip of the spear makes up less than 1 percent of the whole weapon. If you choose sacrifice, hard work, and uncertainties, you too can join the ranks of the elite as a position. If you choose not to, that's OK—you can still be elite at what it is you decide to do. This is not a free ticket to just exist. Life is give and take. You give your time to be compensated in some way or another, whether that be monetary, physical, intellectual, or emotional. Every time you spend that compensation (buying stuff, feeling loved, learning more, getting stronger/faster/better), you agree to the terms of how your time is spent. Don't get angry about your job, relationship, classes, or exercise—do what you agreed to do until you renegotiate terms. Living is giving and taking. Existing is converting oxygen into carbon dioxide, turning chips and soda into poop, and wearing out the channel buttons on your remote.

Get out there and live.

Being at the tip of the spear is volunteerism on steroids. It is a choice to DO and BEHAVE like most people choose not to. No matter your upbringing or your struggles, it's a choice to work harder than you ever thought possible and then work even harder the next day.

The common created the uncommon. Without regular forces, you wouldn't have Special Forces. If there were no normal operations, you wouldn't have special operations. The fact is that the 1 percent needs the 99 percent a lot more than the 99 needs the 1.

I stumbled into this life and stayed for the other 99 percent.

YOU MATTER. I'm just here to make you believe it.

Now, the ball is in your court. Play with it.

ABOUT THE AUTHOR

Rodney Magallan, a respected subject matter expert in protective operations and personal security operations, has vast experience in semi-permissive and non-permissive environments. Over the past thirty-five years, he has served as a Navy SEAL, with the US Marshals Service, with the CIA, and as an executive protection manager in the corporate and private sector.

After completing boot camp and "A" school, he volunteered for Basic Underwater Demolition/SEAL training and graduated with class 143 in July of 1987. His first SEAL command was SEAL Team 4, and he deployed three times before detaching in December 1991. He then attended an Army special forces medical sergeants course and graduated in 1993. CDR Magallan was subsequently selected to serve with SEAL Team 6 with whom he deployed six times. In 1997, he received orders to Special Boat Unit 20 as the senior medical department representative. He was quickly identified to help lead the development and implementation of the maritime craft air delivery system as well as train the sailors who would be operating this new capability. In 2000, he pursued federal law enforcement and affiliated with the naval reserves.

CDR Magallan spent five years in civilian federal service as a deputy US marshal for the Southern District of Texas, a protective agent for the Global Response Staff with the CIA, and the lead instructor responsible for training other protective agents. After, Rodney spent four years as a civilian executive protection specialist. He also gained corporate experience with Walmart and private experience with Watermark.

In 2002, CDR Magallan received his commission as a naval special warfare officer. He was mobilized in 2007 to Combined Joint Task Force – Horn of Africa as the task unit commander. In 2009, he redesignated as a full-time support officer and was assigned to Naval Special Warfare Support Activity Team One. He deployed in 2010 with SEAL Team 3 to Joint Special Operation Task Force – Philippines as a cross-functional team officer in charge. In the subsequent years, CDR Magallan maintained his stellar record of service with SEAL Team 17 and SEAL Team 18 among others, acting as operations officer, commanding officer, or executive officer at different commands. In September of 2021, CDR Magallan retired from US naval service at the rank of commander with the status of honorable service.

CDR Magallan has been awarded the Exceptional Performance Award by the CIA, the Defense Meritorious Service Medal, the Meritorious Service Medal (one gold star), the Joint Service Commendation Medal, the Navy and Marine Corps Commendation Medal (four gold stars), the Joint Service Achievement Medal, the Navy and Marine Corps Achievement Medal (one gold star), the Armed Forces Service Medal, three flag letters of commendation, and various other unit and personal awards.

Rodney Magallan is a level-two instructor certified under CIA University, a Federal Law Enforcement Training Centers firearms instructor (qualified as a weapons expert), and an apprentice instructor in Thai boxing and Kali under Sifu Pat Tray Trident Martial Arts. He resides in Georgetown, Texas, with his loving wife, Veronica; his daughter, Raigan; his son, Evan; and their chihuahua, Jilli Boo.

ENDNOTE

1. Keegan, B., & Lahey, L. L. (2016). *An Everyone Culture* (p. 336). Harvard Business Review Press, 53.